Your
Retirement
Masterplan

If you want to know how ...

Seven Steps to Leaving the Rat Race
Freeing yourself from the 9–5 grind

The Downshifter's Guide to Relocation
Escape to a simpler, less stressful way of life

Setting up and Running Your Own Business
The complete guide to succeeding with a small business

Buying a Property in Spain
An insider guide to finding a home in the sun

Retire Abroad
Your complete guide to a new life in the sun

howtobooks

Please send for a free copy of the latest catalogue to:
How To Books
3 Newtec Place, Magdalen Road
Oxford OX4 1RE, United Kingdom
e-mail: info@howtobooks.co.uk
htttp://www.howtobooks.co.uk

Your Retirement Masterplan

How to ensure you have a fulfilling and enjoyable third age

Jim Green

howtobooks

Published by How To Books Ltd,
3 Newtec Place, Magdalen Road,
Oxford OX4 1RE. United Kingdom.
Tel: (01865) 793806. Fax: (01865) 248780
email: info@howtobooks.co.uk
www.howtobooks.co.uk

British Library Cataloguing in Publication Data.
A catalogue record for this book is available from the British Library.

Produced for How To Books by Deer Park Productions, Tavistock
Cover design by Baseline Arts, Oxford
Typesetting and design by Sparks, Oxford – www.sparks.co.uk
Printed and bound in Great Britain by Cromwell Press, Trowbridge, Wiltshire

NOTE: The material contained in this book is set out in good faith for general guidance and no liability can be accepted for loss or expense incurred as a result of relying in particular circumstances on statements made in this book. Laws and regulations are complex and liable to change, and readers should check the current position with the relevant authorities before making personal arrangements.

Contents

Illustrations

Preface

Years ago you gave up working at 65, and that was pretty much it. Nowadays there is an entirely new concept of retirement. It is a new beginning that opens up a whole new age, as you enter the third plateau of the lifespan. You may make of it what you will, because you have choices. You can flounder through the rest of your life without goals and suffer the emptiness of achieving very little, or you can let someone else set your goals for you and endure the frustration of living the life someone else wants you to. Alternatively, you can set your own retirement goals and experience the profound truth expressed by Robert Browning when he said, 'Grow old along with me! The best is yet to be.'

The choice is yours.

The purpose of this book is to show you how to identify the keys to a happy and successful retirement, how to set your own exclusive goals, and how to create a masterplan for actualisation on the higher plane. There is no one way to enjoy retirement, since we are all unique. Whatever the nature of your personal goals, and no matter how and when you wish to retire, you owe it to yourself to chart your own course with confidence and with your authentic self as a priority. The essence of your planning must be to capture the 'new retirement' archetype, which is about renewal: a transition to new beginnings, new options, and new opportunities.

Throughout the text you will find a multitude of links to resources designed to help you get the best out of your third-age years. For your added convenience, many of these links are repeated by category in the international retirement directory at the end of this book.

1

The secret of the three little boxes

This book focuses on the *heart* of planning ahead for a happy and successful retirement. In it, you will find no more than occasional references to financial scheduling. Why? For two reasons. First, there is a plethora of other available tomes that specialise in the topic. Second, because the die has already been cast, we either choose to exercise prudence during our working lives or we don't. But, however we decide to handle our finances as we contemplate retirement, we would do well to give attention to the benchmarks for enjoying a fulfilling and enriching third age on the *higher plane*.

Equally, you will find that there is only a passing mention of physical jerks in this book. Keeping fit starts in the mind, so concentrate on keeping that in good order, and your body will quickly find its own levels of well-being.

What you will find are tried-and-tested templates that you can adjust, according to your inclinations and irrespective of your financial standing, to produce a masterplan for achieving a successful and rewarding future. That is what retirement is: the future, the beginning of the rest of your life. And it would appear that it is never too soon to start on the plan. There is one website (www.drummondmoores.com) that offers retirement planning advice to 20-year-olds ...

The new concept of retirement

The whole notion of retirement has taken on a new complexion, an entirely new definition. Previously people thought of retirement as the beginning of the end. Today we regard retirement as a new beginning, a transition that can be accurately described as a spiritual and temporal *renewal*. Retiring doesn't automatically mean entering a traditional retirement lifestyle, where the main focus is on rest and leisure.

The traditional retirement lifestyle is but one of many options available to the enlightened person who is transitioning from current employment. And retirement doesn't mean you are finished; it means you are just beginning. Yet, old ideas still persist, even in the most unlikely circumstances. On the eve of his 80th birthday, Lord 'Dickie' Attenborough was asked by an interviewer if he had any thoughts of retiring. He replied, 'Not at all. The thought of retirement is anathema to me. I can't imagine anything worse.' Were the great man to opt for idleness he might well be right, but he has alternatives (as we all do) to carve out a retirement chock-full of interest and fulfilment. And veteran television reporter Charles Wheeler (also 80) was said to have claimed, in the 15–21 November 2003 issue of the *Radio Times*, that 'Retiring means you age quickly. Also you lose contact with people. Working keeps your brain alive.' Wrong, Charles, retirement neither makes you grow old nor is it the cause of losing contacts. But right, Charles, work does ensure that the intellect keeps ticking over – and that is part of the secret of the three little boxes.

Today's retirees don't fade away into obscurity

The old notion of retirement was that it started at the age of 65, and then you pretty much stopped. Today the average retirement age is 57.5 years, and retirees want nothing to do with stopping. They aren't looking to fade away, they don't want to be couch potatoes; they want to find rewarding activities, they want enriching endeavours. Certainly they want leisure, and naturally they want to have fun. But essentially they seek fulfilment: their own sense of purpose and meaning. They want something new, something different, perhaps something original, and definitely something interesting at a deep personal level.

Career transition

People approaching their first retirement transition need exactly the same process of self-analysis and sound consultation that they would receive from a competent career consultant if they were going through a job change. As job changers need to generate their career options in a clear and understandable way, so pre-retirees need the same options-generation process but with slightly different content, slightly different goals, and an entirely different purpose.

The great experiment

Two separate trends are converging to create the greatest demographic experiment we have ever seen. First, people are retiring earlier than ever before. Second, people are living longer. The longevity of our total population continues to rise. Today, males can expect to live an average of 77 years, while females can expect to live almost five years longer. Every indication is that these numbers will continue to rise. The UK 2001 census showed that for the first time ever *there are more people over 60 than there are children*. Having been static in the 1970s, the overall population has begun to grow again. The rate of increase is in line with other European countries, but significantly slower than the rate in the US or Australia. This new wave is silently sweeping our society.

We are ageing. No, not just individually, we are all doing this; but culturally in our society, in our population, we are also ageing. This process can be seen in two ways. First, the number of maturing persons is growing faster than any other segment of our population. Second, the proportion of the overall population that is over 65 years of age is also growing, and indeed it is predicted that it will account for 23 per cent of the entire UK populace by 2025. We are getting older both absolutely and relatively. But this isn't a tragedy for our culture. On the contrary, it is a bonanza if we can truly squeeze from our retirement years all the potential for personal and individual achievement that is there; if we can aim to be all that we can be.

Third-age people form a unique group

They are healthier by far, wealthier to varying degrees, better educated, and more skilled; they have vitality, verve, desire, and personal direction, and they have deeper insight than our society has heretofore experienced. The group, if they can be seen as a group, is a power-packed potential of achievement, practical problem-solving, enlightened wisdom, and focused energy. Here is one of the most pressing challenges of our time; here is where our pioneering spirit of exploring new territory can manifest itself in ways never before possible. The challenge is how to harness the phenomenal resources resident in this talented, resourceful, seasoned, and purpose-filled population we call retirees.

Age doesn't guarantee a fulfilling retirement

Age alone offers no guarantee that we'll gather the necessary wisdom to exploit the opportunities of retirement and find contentment. Nor does age miraculously give us the requisite tools, competencies, knowledge, and attitudinal shifts that will ensure that retirement will proceed maximally. Some people have 30 years of experience, and others have 1 year of experience 30 times over. Nor does retirement necessarily mean cessation from all work. The answer lies in the secret of the three little boxes of life, which calls for some work in our preparations for a happy and successful retirement.

The journey from full-time work to full-time retirement in its traditional sense may take a year or so to accomplish, but there is no rush. The question for pre-retirees during this time is to what degree they are actively and consciously encountering the personal growth tasks and individual challenges that need to be addressed in order to achieve the maturity necessary to really get the most out of retirement.

Different strokes for different folks

Some retirees embrace their new lifestyle generously. They seem to revel in their new-found freedom, thrive in their new activities and new relationships, and celebrate in their good fortune to be alive in this marvellous time of life. Others appear indifferent about retirement. While not downhearted, they seem uneasy, slightly distressed, and occasionally irritable beyond what could be considered normal. Still other retirees are repelled by the uncertainties or by the monotony of a life that seems to them empty of challenge, action, and excitement. Something has drained from them; they appear to be simply surviving, not genuinely thriving in their new life. Certain people whom one may think are the most prepared to take the plunge into retirement turn out to be the very ones who find the retirement-lifestyle road to be the roughest. At some level they are resisting the changes that retirement brings. They resist in many ways, with denial, avoidance, anger, irritability, depression, submission, and so on.

Addressing the perplexing question

This brings us to a somewhat perplexing question: 'What is retirement supposed to be?' Is it marked down to be a time of rest, a new career path, a playground, withdrawal, new stimulation, respite, or what? There is tremendous ambiguity surrounding retirement. We really don't know exactly what it is supposed to entail, and there are few, if any, social directives in our culture that guide us in organising our retirement with stability. And yet there is great hope inherent in retiring from workaday pressures; hope for new life prospects, new life directions, new endeavours. Retirement is starting all over again. In a very real sense, retirement is like leaving school behind, but it is also a new beginning of something that is much bigger than any of us can conceive.

Debunking popular myths concerning retirement

This new beginning can be hampered somewhat, though, by taking heed of popular myths spread willy-nilly about the third plateau of the lifespan. Here are four examples that tend to crop up when people talk of the retirement process. Take them at face value, because that is all they are worth.

Myth 1: 'Most people retire because they see themselves getting old'

There is a big difference between getting old and being old. Ask yourself, 'How old would I be if I didn't know how old I was?' And society doesn't help. It tells us we are old if we have a wrinkle or two, and then tries to sell us a restorative unguent or panacea. Can you plan to move along the developmental path with wisdom and not become overly concerned with chronological age? Can you see yourself as timeless, ageless?

Myth 2: 'When people have others who are dependent on them, they tend to retire earlier rather than later'

In reality, when we have others dependent on us, we tend to put life on hold. Decisions about retirement and lifestyle are postponed in order to continue to support others financially, physically, or emotionally. Baby boomers (also known as the sandwich generation) are often dealing with childcare and eldercare issues simultaneously. When a 57-year-old male has a teenage child and elderly parents, demands on him are huge. He may find it easier to postpone a work-related decision until something changes with his dependants or until a change is forced upon him. What can you do to plan for potential dependant issues, or how can you change your current situation to move towards your retirement goals?

Myth 3: 'One of the best ways genuinely to enjoy your retirement is to be free from everything you previously experienced in your job'

Although it is tempting to discard many things related to your work, it is very important to replace the five functions of work: financial remuneration, time management, utility or sense of purpose, status, and socialisation. *The need for these five benefits from work doesn't go away simply because we retire.* They have become such a part of our lives that we can't simply discard them without with some emotional, psychological, or spiritual consequences. These factors become requirements. How you replace the benefits received from work is crucial. Can you create a plan to do this?

Myth 4: 'Men find it more difficult than women to adjust to retirement'

Gender doesn't play a role in retirement adjustment. What makes a difference is finding a life direction for retirement that offers you a driving purpose and a deep sense of personal fulfilment. What gives your life meaning? A directed and purposeful life can lead to a healthier and happier retirement.

What plans do you put in place right now?

With these misconceptions clarified, what are you going to do to make your retirement a success? What plans can you put in place right now to ensure an enjoyable and productive retirement? What is your definition of a happy and successful retirement? The answers to these questions begin to emerge when you unravel the secret of the three little boxes ...

The secret unravelled

Society preordains the pattern our lives will take, and places it in a linear sequence comprising three neat little boxes demarcated by age grading (Fig. 1.1).

Fig. 1.1 The three little boxes of life

We are destined to conform to this pattern in respect of the first two boxes, but do we need to slope tentatively into the third without quantifiable expectations or a plan for fulfilment? No, we don't. The secret of the three little boxes is to retain the most fulfilling aspects of the first two boxes, carry them forward with you into the third box, and combine the disparate functions of all three productively in the twilight years.

I will show you how to merge these functions seamlessly to provide a happy and successful retirement. I will also let you in on the secrets that keep me and other active retirees busy, satisfied, and fulfilled. There is work to be done but it will be worthwhile. In the process you will learn:

o how to identify the success patterns inherent in a rewarding retirement;

o how to maintain the edge by recognising trends, so that you can anticipate rather than react to change; and o how to use this wisdom to shape your own destiny in the third age.

Being ahead of the wave, rather than behind it, is the better place to be in retirement.

Planning a happy and successful retirement

There is a lot to think about when you retire.

o How will I spend my time?
o What will I be able to afford?
o How can I best sort out my finances?
o Do I want to do any form of work?
o If so, will the work be paid or voluntary?
o What sort of activities will I be suited to, given my experience and temperament?
o What sort of hobbies will suit me?
o Do I want to get some more education?
o Where can I find the necessary information?

In the chapters to follow, we will focus on charting a route to a happy and successful retirement (Fig. 1.2).

Learning how to enjoy a fulfilling and enriching third age is to exceed the wildest expectations of youth. Let's go …

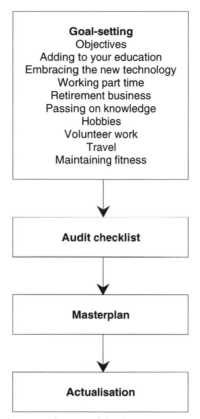

Fig. 1.2 The route to a happy and successful retirement

2

Identifying the keys to a happy and successful retirement

Before we identify the keys to a happy and successful retirement, let us edge around a few talking points surrounding the entire process of entering the third and final plateau of the lifespan. Most of us get anxious as retirement looms, and it is as well to face facts before someone else thrusts them uncomfortably in our direction.

What do I need to enjoy the retirement years?

What you need is a plan; a plan of your own devising. There is no single standard formula for success, because each individual must decide for themself how they want to live during the retirement years. Everyone must prepare for the emotional, physical, and financial realities of retirement, but fortunately the number of resources to help shape one's plan is increasing every day.

Identify the keys, set your goals, tap into the resources, and the plan will take care of itself, as you will realise when we reach Chapter 14.

What will the future hold?

Sixty-eight per cent of respondents in a recent US government survey had no formal preparation for retirement. What type of planning did they consider most important? Financial planning, answered 24.3 per cent, but a surprising 23 per cent indicated that *developing interests to pursue in retirement* was most important.

One big mistake that many people make is assuming that retirement is going to be a continuation of the old life. But it isn't really a holiday from the work world, because you won't return there full time. It will involve major changes in the routine that governed every aspect of your life. Once you retire, you will have 45 to 50 hours a week of extra free time. Even the most absorbing of hobbies and interests may not fill that time entirely.

As you plan for retirement, plan for future fulfilment. Think through your ideal post-retirement day, in *specifics*, not generalities. Begin to develop interests and activities that will provide you with a variety of pursuits in retirement, from hobbies and further education, through voluntary or part-time work, to starting a small business for pleasure or profit.

What about financial planning?

You can't retire without the financial means to support yourself. This doesn't mean, however, that you have to be independently wealthy. With solid financial planning and realistic saving-and-investment goals, it is entirely possible to retire and maintain an adequate standard of living. Even if all you have to live on is your state pension, you can still make a go of it. Although it is never easy when money is tight, many retirees make an admirable fist of their financial limitations. When you plan for achievement, anything is possible.

Many financial planners and investment advisers market services whereby they evaluate your current situation and make recommendations to you.

o You will need an overview of your current net worth.
o You will want objective advice about the ways you can increase your net worth to achieve an acceptable income during your retirement years.

Here's a cautionary note: make sure that you are under no obligation to purchase any stocks, insurance, or other products from the person who prepares your plan. Investigate carefully any financial consultant you are considering before you begin a relationship. Friends and colleagues may be a good source of referrals.

In any case, always consult works of reference to help you plan and evaluate your retirement finances. Your local public library contains many helpful books about financial planning for retirement. Read about your options – and the earlier the better.

How much should I save?

Deciding how much money you need for retirement is obviously a highly personal calculation. It depends on any number of factors, from your current lifestyle to your general state of health. Arriving at finite conclusions is no easy

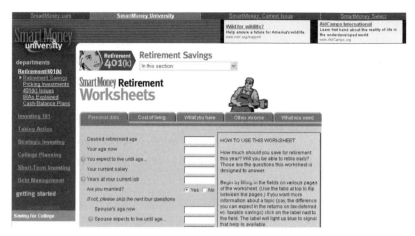

Fig. 2.1 Online worksheets to help you plan your retirement savings

matter, and that is why www.smartmoneyuniversity.com has designed a free set of interactive worksheets to let you tailor your estimate according to your own circumstances (Figure 2.1).

These worksheets will take a little while to complete. But when you are done, you will have a dependable estimate of how much money you will need in retirement – whether you retire early or late – and how much you will need to save this year to reach that goal.

What the worksheets won't tell you is what to save five years from now, or even next year. By then, anything from your circumstances to your market outlook might have changed. That means you should take the time to repeat this planning exercise every couple of years – or every year as you near retirement. I began to use these worksheets a few years before my own retirement, and found the application extremely useful.

What about pensions?

Many retirees have private pension plans; many more don't. If you fall into the latter category, your state pension income will depend on how much you contributed during your working life, and whether or not you contracted into or out of the state earnings-related pension scheme (SERPS).

If you are more than four months from the official retirement age, you can apply to have a state pension forecast by visiting www.inlandrevenue.gov/uk and completing the online form. This forecast will show your pension, based on your circumstances at the time, and will include details of any additional pension, contracted-out income, or graduated retirement benefit that you are entitled to. If you are widowed or divorced, your late or former spouse's national insurance contributions can sometimes be used to get you a better pension. Further information not covered by your pension forecast will be sent to you separately.

If, on the other hand, you are fortunate enough to have a company pension to draw upon, and are either recently retired or about to retire, you should consider the following essential factors in your retirement planning.

Company pension statement

Is your pension what you expected? Check that your company pension statement correctly records your personal details, such as:

o your name and address;
o your date of birth;
o your marital status;
o the name(s) of your spouse(s), if any;

o the name(s) of your child(ren), if any;
o the date you entered a company pension scheme; and
o the date you left a company pension scheme.

Final-salary pension scheme

What type of company pension scheme do you belong to? In a final-salary pension scheme, your pension is calculated by multiplying your years in the scheme by the accrual rate (usually a 60th of your final salary). If you belong to a final-salary pension scheme, you would be wise to check:

o how final salary is defined;
o what is excluded (for example, overtime);
o whether the final salary includes the whole salary or the salary less the lower earnings limit; and
o what the accrual rate of your scheme is.

Money-purchase pension scheme

In a money-purchase pension scheme, you and your employer put money into a fund, the performance of which determines the size of your pension. The fund can fluctuate in value with stock-market movements. All additional voluntary contribution (AVC) funds are related to money-purchase pension schemes.

Contracted-in and contracted-out pension schemes

In a contracted-out pension scheme (that is, a company pension scheme that has contracted out of SERPS), you pay less national insurance and don't receive the additional state pension at the official retirement age. Instead, you receive an equivalent amount from your company as part of your company pension. In a contracted-in pension scheme (that is, a company pension scheme that has contracted into SERPS), you pay the usual amount of national insurance and receive the additional state pension at the official retirement age.

State make-up

In some company pension schemes, your company pension is reduced when you reach the official retirement age and take your state pension. It means that your income doesn't increase by very much at the official retirement age, but effectively you have enjoyed a better pension up to that time. Check in your pension booklet to see if this applies to your scheme.

Pay day

Company pension schemes may pay on the same day as your salary used to be paid or on a different day. Check when your scheme pays, in case your bank balance is 'compromised' soon after you leave work.

Payslips

Many company pension schemes don't send out payslips every month because of the cost. You may only get one when your pension varies by more than a certain amount from the month before.

Tax office

Check if your tax office will change when you start claiming your company pension.

Changes in your circumstances

Make sure your company pension scheme administrators know if you move address or alter your marital status. If you change the bank account to which they transfer the pension, let them know.

Tax

Your pension will be taxed according to the tax code issued by the Inland Revenue. If this is wrong, you may pay too much or too little tax. It is up to you to check your coding. If you have other sources of income, make sure the tax allowances are set against your main income. At the official retirement age, your tax code will change, so that the tax on your state pension is recovered from your company pension.

Company pension increases

By how much does your company pension increase each year? Private-sector pensions must be increased by a minimum amount by law, usually 3 per cent or the rate of inflation, whichever is the lower. Many private-sector pension schemes also top up the payment to approach or match inflation. The top-ups are at the discretion of the trustees of the scheme, and aren't automatic. You should be able to see a record of increases if you ask.

If your pension scheme has contracted out of SERPS, your company will make increases on most of your pension, but the SERPS element (known as the guaranteed minimum pension) will be linked to the retail price index (RPI) by the government once you reach the official retirement age. Most public-sector pension schemes are RPI-linked.

Working beyond retirement

You can continue to work beyond retirement and still receive your company pension. All income is added together for tax purposes, and you are taxed accordingly. There is no tax disadvantage in getting extra income – the more you earn, the more you get, even though it is taxed.

Company pensions from previous employers

If you have deferred company pensions from previous employers, get a statement from them indicating what pension might be payable, when it can be paid, and if there are any commutation rights (that is, options to commute part of the pension into tax-free cash). In other words, ask the same questions that you do of your current company pension scheme. Legislation now allows greater flexibility in the treatment of preserved company pensions than may have been the case when you left company pension schemes. If you have lost track of the company with whom you had the pension, or the company has ceased trading or gone bankrupt, you can still find the pension from one of the following addresses:

- o The Registrar of Pension Funds Occupational Pensions Board, PO Box 1NN, Newcastle-upon-Tyne NE99 1NN. Tel: 0191 225 6398.
- o Occupational Pensions Advisory Service, 11 Belgrave Road, London SW1V 1RB. Tel: 0171 233 8080.

You can also get help from an independent financial adviser or through the Citizens' Advice Bureau.

In case of death

Check that the beneficiaries you have nominated in both your current and previous company pensions are still according to your wishes. This is especially important if your personal circumstances have changed, perhaps due to marriage or divorce. The 'Expression of Wish' or 'Nomination' form should be filled in. This indicates to the trustees whom you wish to benefit from any payments due from the company pension fund in the event of your death. You can change the names of your beneficiaries at any time.

Dependants' pensions

When a pensioner dies, the surviving spouse will normally receive a dependant's pension. In most company pension schemes, the dependant's pension is half of the employee's pension (see also 'Five-year guarantee' below), and the dependant's pension is not affected if part of the pension is commuted into tax-free cash. However, check the arrangements of your own company pension scheme – there are some variations. The dependant's pension will normally be paid to a spouse or partner, but some schemes only pay to legally married partners. There may also be restrictions if the partnership is of short duration or if there is a large age difference. Children may also benefit from a dependant's pension if they are below a certain age. Again, make sure to check the arrangements of your scheme.

Five-year guarantee

Most company pensions are guaranteed to be paid for five years after a person retires. This means that if a pensioner dies within the five years, the balance of money that would have been due is paid to the surviving spouse as a tax-free sum. The dependant's pension normally starts on death. There can be variations, so check what your own company pension scheme does.

How can I diminish the disadvantages of retirement?

In her book *When Women Retire: The Problems They Face and How to Solve Them* (Crown Publishers, 1992), author Carole Sinclair advises, 'If a job gives your life structure, plan to replace that structure in retirement.' In terms of fulfilment, it is important to understand that many people, both men and women, receive a great deal besides a pay cheque from their jobs. Job-related benefits, aside from income and cash flow, include:

o a structure to one's life;
o intellectual challenges;
o a sense of self-worth and accomplishment; and
o the camaraderie that comes from working with other people.

Are you certain you are ready for retirement? Surveys show that many people who retire don't really want to, so take careful stock of whether you are prepared to lose the structure and other benefits of the working world. If you are forcibly retired or are unhappy in your current job, you have other alternatives than a lifetime of unstructured leisure. Now more than ever, older adults are heading back to college, or into other careers, or into voluntary work after their long-term careers end.

Here are just a few options to consider.

o Keep on working if you can, by staying on at your job past the age of 65 or beginning in a new career.
o Work part-time either with your present employer or at another company.
o Do voluntary work for fulfilment, for example, at a local school, hospital, or cultural institution. Once you are bitten by the volunteering bug, you may well find one type of voluntary work leads to another. The emotional and intellectual rewards can be tremendous.
o Start your own business.

Retirement will change your life completely. In particular, it will increase your leisure time. Your happiness therefore depends on understanding your own needs, and structuring both time and activity to meet those needs.

General keys to a happy and successful retirement

The most important aspect of adjusting to retirement is planning for a smooth transition. You would do well to start by identifying the general keys to a happy and successful retirement. Some examples of general keys are identified below.

1 Practise living on your estimated retirement income after deductions, say for business expenses.

2 Start developing some of the retirement activities you think will interest you. There are contacts to make and research to undertake, whether you have in mind voluntary work, further education, a second career, or starting a business.

3 If you plan to move, learn everything you can about your prospective new home patch. It isn't likely that you will be able to move repeatedly, nor would you want to, so spend time if you can in the new neighbourhood. Talk to people who live there; keep looking for disadvantages. You already know the advantages because they are what attracted you in the first place.

4 Strengthen relationships outside the working environment – with family, friends, and neighbours.

5 Check how long it takes you to perform various activities around the house or garden; chores that you look forward to doing in retirement. You may think there are enough everyday jobs to keep you busy forever, but you will probably zip right through them in a few weeks and then have to start looking for something else to keep you fully occupied.

6 Involve any spouse or partner in your retirement plans. This is just as important as working out a viable financial future. Couples who have lived together in the evenings, at weekends, and during holidays for virtually all their lives don't necessarily find it easy, especially at first, to be together all day, every day. You and your significant other might want to talk together about seemingly minor potential irritants.

Specific keys to a happy and successful retirement

Your ability to handle stress in this phase of life isn't only a key to longevity, but also a foundation for a fulfilling journey in the third age. Researchers have identified core lifestyle attributes that are present in happy and successful retirees, and in individuals who have stress-proof personalities. These attributes include:

o taking and maintaining control over the principal elements in their lives;

o being committed to living each day to the full;

o challenging themselves to learn new things and create new activities; and

o connecting freely with family, friends, and community.

The identification of specific keys (that is, core lifestyle attributes that relate to you personally) is germane to happiness and success in retirement. Some examples of specific keys are identified below.

1 Having a positive attitude towards ageing and life transitions

Our ability to roll with the punches is a key factor in stress management. There are life transitions that we can expect in retirement; sociologists have identified at least six separate life transitions in the retirement phase alone. Coupled with the predictable changes are those unpredictable life events that take the best-laid plans and blow them asunder. Perhaps the greatest transition of all is the one that we see each time we look in a mirror and see ourselves age. It is easy to forget that ageing needn't feature in our minds.

2 Having strong visions and values

The foundation of a happy and successful retirement is an understanding of what the primary aim of life is. This gives us our sense of purpose and defines fulfilment in our activities, relationships, health, and money matters. If we don't have a sense of purpose, what gets us up in the morning? The concept of 'living on purpose' is a great descriptor of a happy and successful retirement. Our life dreams, and the goals that we set to give our life meaning, come from this life purpose.

3 Subscribing to healthy ageing

If we don't feel good about our lives or ourselves, we undermine all of the other factors that may be in place in a happy and successful retirement. The most important element of healthy ageing is our mental outlook rather than our physical state. Well-being refers more to how we view our physical fitness than to whether we are actually physically fit. In retirement, stress management becomes a crucial element of healthy ageing.

4 Having a positive definition of work

Our work is the thing that we do to contribute our skills, experience, labour, or knowledge to society in some way. Even when we leave the traditional workplace, we still have a need to share our administrative strengths and transferable skills. Finally, if we have a positive attitude towards the workplace, then the desire to have a retirement free from any kind of employment becomes irrelevant. A wise person once said, 'If you love what you do, you never have to work again!'

5 Nurturing familial and marital relationships

In general, we need close familial relationships. Our relationships define us, give us a purpose for living our lives, and force us to create life goals. They can also act as external controllers when we find ourselves in the midst of marital or familial discord. Researchers have found that people in satisfying personal relationships have fewer illnesses and better overall health.

6 Having a supportive social network

We all have a basic need to share our lives, experiences, and temporal journey with those closest to us. In retirement, our friendships and close relationships may offer us the validation that we received in the workplace. Those relationships give us the opportunity to connect on many levels with someone close, and to share ourselves. Psychologists have identified our desire to share ourselves as a basic human need. This need is often satisfied in the activities that we enjoy with our friends and wider social network.

7 Engaging in meaningful activities and leisure

Leisure is a fundamental human need. We use it to recharge our batteries, to act as a diversion in our lives, to create excitement and anticipation, or simply to rest and contemplate. Things change, however, when leisure becomes the central focus of our lives. Leisure, by its very nature, loses its lustre when it is the norm in our life rather than the diversion. For many retirees, the idea of leisure is associated with not having to do anything. A lack of stimulation affects our mental and emotional state, and ultimately our physical well-being.

There is a big difference between time-filling activities and the fulfilling activities that we look forward to. In retirement, leisure activities often replace workplace functions to meet the basic needs that we have.

8 Enjoying financial comfort

Some retirees feel that a happy and successful retirement is guaranteed by financial security. However, there is no price tag on a happy and successful retirement. Financial comfort refers to retirees being able to manage their lives in a satisfying and fulfilling way by using the resources they have. If financial discomfort contributes to retirement stress, then this element isn't in place. Many retirees are able to enjoy happiness despite having far less than others, simply because they have the ability to cut their coat according to their cloth.

When it is someone else's retirement under review

Perhaps the retirement you need to plan for most isn't your own – it may be that of your spouse or partner. How can you minimise the stress on your relationship?

o Be sure to plan finances together. Money planning will cushion stress and help you develop a realistic picture of your future.
o Plan separate activities to assure privacy for each other. Respect each other's routines, friends, and conversations.
o At the same time, develop some common interests, from hobbies through sports to work on a political or community campaign. Such activities help stimulate each other's involvement, and assure you of continuing things to talk about and plan for.

o Keep your lines of communication open. In retirement, you will be talking with each other more than ever before.

Personal case study

When I retired, I had no notion of the keys to a happy and successful retirement. For the first few months I drifted around aimlessly, and then one winter's evening, as I gazed at the rain lashing against the window of my living room, I thought, 'Is this it? Is this the way I'm going to spend the rest of my life, with nothing to do and nowhere to go?' That was my wake-up call. It goaded me into establishing some hazy initial goals and creating a plan of action for fulfilment. It was sometime later before I stumbled across the keys, but not too late to make vital adjustments. You won't have that problem because, before you begin your preparations for a happy and successful retirement, you are already in possession of the keys that open the doors.

3

How to set goals for your new way of life

Now it is time to start setting your goals in position – but not the plan. We'll leave that until after we have reviewed all of your options for enactment. No two people have exactly the same aspirations for impending retirement, so your goals and hence your plan of action will hinge on how you decide to mix and match the activities inherent in the three little boxes of life. *Don't be tempted to discard the first two boxes completely and plunge headlong into the third box.* If you do, you will almost certainly live to regret it.

You have choices that will determine the quality of your life in retirement. As stated previously, you have three main alternatives.

1 You can flounder through the rest of your life without goals and suffer the emptiness of achieving very little.

2 You can let someone else set your goals for you and endure the frustration of living the life someone else wants you to.

3 You can set your own retirement goals and experience the profound truth expressed by Robert Browning when he said, 'Grow old along with me! The best is yet to be.'

The choice is yours.

Steps and stairs to goal-setting

1 Clarify your objectives.
2 Expand your education.
3 Embrace new technology.
4 Consider working part-time.
5 Start your own business.
6 Pass on your knowledge.
7 Develop new hobbies.
8 Do voluntary work.
9 Travel and broaden your perspective.
10 Instigate a personal fitness regime.
11 Cultivate your sense of humour.
12 Think positively about the future.

In addition to signifying opportunity and challenge, retirement for most of us also means freedom and an era in which to follow our chosen pursuits. It is probably the first time in our lives when we get to control our daily, weekly, monthly, and yearly timetables, and, more importantly, to choose the content. The Monday-to-Friday grind is over, as are weekends in the traditional sense; the week becomes a continuous roll-over. We believe that it is a time for careful assessment of our future needs and for preparation to achieve our personal goals. Given an adequate income and good health, the opportunities facing retirees are virtually infinite. We can study a multitude of subjects, take up new hobbies and interests, or become more involved in existing ones. We can start a second career of our choice or volunteer our services to some of the many and varied organisations that help within our communities. This new-found freedom means that we have more time to spend with our families and friends, perhaps giving them the benefit of our lifetime experiences or helping them in a more practical fashion while they are still caught up in the daily grind of work coupled with domestic responsibilities.

Clarify your objectives

Only you can decide on the mix of activities best suited to your ideal of a happy and successful retirement. Review the options in this chapter and elsewhere in the book, and add some of your own. Then set about clarifying your objectives, so that by the time we reach Chapter 14 you will be ready to formulate your plan of enactment. You might start off by stringing together a list of energetic projects around the house: painting and decorating, rewiring, converting the loft, adding a conservatory, or whatever. While all of these may be admirable aspirations, be aware that they won't keep you totally occupied. You would also do well to search within yourself on the higher plane.

Expand your education

There are many opportunities for retirees who have a desire to learn something new. Why not work towards a degree in something that has always interested you? Or if working towards a degree sounds too stressful (it wasn't for a 90-year-old, as you will learn in the next chapter), why not just take a few courses? Classes are accessible everywhere from the Open University to your local community centre. In Chapter 4, we will discuss some of the options open to you, as we uncover the reasons why it is never too late to learn something new. Perhaps you'd like to read music, master a new language, or brush up your hobby skills. Wherever your interest lies, there is a course available that is just right for you.

Embrace new technology

If you have yet to come to terms with the information age, now is time to make a start. You don't even need to own a computer to get up to speed. Moreover, in Chapter 4, we will examine the advantages of participating in the People's Network for free at your local public library. Does the thought of using a computer for gratification fill you with feelings of dread? Don't let it. There is plenty of assistance on tap to enable you to become proficient in next to no time.

Consider working part-time

Many people when they retire discover very quickly that they miss the companionship they enjoyed whilst working full-time. If you fall into this category, think about taking up the cudgels again on a part-time basis. Would it be feasible to go back to your old job working a few days a week, or would you prefer to try your hand at something completely different? Would the extra cash come in handy? The trick is to treat part-time involvement as just one of the cogs in your overall plan for a happy and successful retirement. Chapter 6 will provide some opportunities for exploration and show you how other retirees are handling the option of working part-time.

Start your own business

Why would you want to do that? For much the same reason as going back to work part-time. I have done it, several times over, but this time it is different. I don't report to anyone and my involvement is strictly part-time, allowing me to indulge in other retirement interests. Have you ever thought about starting your own business? Have you ever taken the trouble to find out what it entails? It isn't something you should undertake without due consideration and, certainly not in retirement, without a thorough grounding. In Chapter 7 we will look at how this works in practice and what you must do in preparation should the prospect appeal to you.

Pass on your knowledge

In retirement, there are few loftier ideals you can pursue than passing on the knowledge, wisdom, and experience that you gleaned in your own working life. You could achieve this on a one-to-one basis as a voluntary tutor, in the ways described in Chapter 8, or you could produce a self-help book or create a dedicated website to mete out your expertise. Do you perhaps consider that the latter options might prove to be beyond your capability? Chapter 9 suggests novel ways for accomplishment.

Develop new hobbies

Retirement is a wonderful time to develop new hobbies or delve more deeply into those you have enjoyed in the past. Hobbies are much more than just ways to pass the time – they can be a rich source of personal satisfaction, an avenue to meet new people, and an opportunity for creativity. If during your working life you were involved in a calling that was more of a pleasurable pastime than a job, you are indeed fortunate; you just carry on doing what you did with increasing satisfaction. Artists, writers, and musicians fall into this category. Not everyone is that blessed though, so take advantage of your retirement to explore, select, and develop hobbies that will fulfil your rightful expectations. Chapter 10 provides more than 50 retirement hobbies for your perusal and consideration.

Do voluntary work

If working part-time for monetary gain holds no appeal for you in retirement, then consider giving your services freely to some worthwhile causes. If you were a teacher, perhaps you could help adults and children with learning difficulties; if you were a skilled tradesman, perhaps you could give school-leavers a start. But you don't need to be a skilled worker to become involved. The avenues for providing urgently needed assistance are boundless, and various voluntary work possibilities are explored in Chapter 8.

Travel and broaden your perspective

When you are retired, you can arrange holidays in the quieter seasons, taking advantage of cheaper prices and a wider selection of resorts. Long sunny breaks to escape the cold British winter are an option. Equally, you might wish to investigate the wonders just around the corner on our sceptred isle. Chapter 12 provides you with a composite retirement holiday planner.

Instigate a personal fitness regime

Is this how you keep fit?

o Watching TV hour after hour each evening?
o Driving around the supermarket precinct several times looking for a close parking spot, rather than disembarking some distance away from the store and walking?
o Driving down the road to post a letter, rather than walking or riding your bike to the postbox?
o Passing up a round of golf to sit at home and watch the pros play on TV?

These habits can shorten your life. Exercise on the other hand will make a huge difference in the way you feel. The best exercises are walking (three times a week for 30 minutes, preferably on alternate days) cycling, and swimming. Why not also try some activities that combine exercise and fun, for example, dancing or gardening? Chapter 11 looks at ways and means of toning up for a healthy lifestyle in retirement.

Cultivate your sense of humour

Cultivating your sense of humour in retirement enables you to be more open to change and more interested in the world around you. Nurture your environment, your friends, and your interests, and try to do so with a smile for everyone and everything. It works.

Think positively about the future

Above all think positively about your retirement. You have engaged, or are about to engage, in the most exciting and rewarding time of your life. Clarify your objectives, set your goals in position, formulate your plan – and go for it ...

Personal case study

Here is how I interpreted my own personal goals, what happened thereafter, and what's still happening seven years into 'retirement' ...

Objectives

My objectives remained unaltered after belatedly discovering the keys to a happy and successful retirement. All I wanted were peace, quiet, and a sense of achievement and fulfilment In everything I would tackle in my advancing years. I had already sampled most of the material things life has to offer, but no longer had need of them, save for a few modest indulgences. You know what they say: *less is more*, and it is true.

Further education

Now, further education was something I both wanted and needed. None of us live long enough to learn how to cross the road properly, and I immediately embarked upon (and am still pursuing) a series of further education courses.

Technology

Mastering new technology was high on my list of priorities. I had founded and managed many businesses during my career without access to computers, mobile communications, or the internet. I leapt into this learning curve with enthusiasm and have progressed far enough in my researches to produce a best-selling book, *Starting an Internet Business at Home* (Kogan Page, 2001).

Part-time work

I had a stab at part-time work in between projects, but found it less than fulfilling, mainly because I'm not very good (nor ever was) at being subjected to supervision. It didn't suit me in retirement, but it does several of my friends – and it might just work for you.

Starting a business

Starting a business was something I couldn't resist, because I had been doing it for most of my working life and had even written a book on the subject. Currently, I have several internet enterprises and am in the throes of developing more. Think about it for yourself, even if you have never before considered running a business. Online or offline, it could prove to be a great new rewarding adventure in retirement.

Passing on knowledge

I pass on knowledge wherever and whenever I can, and I operate a website (www.writing-for-profit.com) chock-full of tried-and-tested strategies for writers aspiring to publication in the realms of niche non-fiction.

Hobbies

Academically I was considered doltish in my schooldays, but I had a passion for art. Today one of my core retirement activities is watercolour painting, with the accent being on landscapes and architecture.

Voluntary work

I do my stint of voluntary work, here and there, on causes close to my heart.

Travel

I travelled the world several times over during my career and have no desire to repeat the exercise. Instead, I get my kicks from short-hop stays in the Lake District.

Fitness levels

Physical jerks aren't my scene, but I enjoy a brisk 30-minute walk on alternate days.

Humour

Cultivating a healthy sense of humour becomes easier as I get older. Events that enraged me in my younger days only evoke a wry smile now.

Positive thinking

Knock me over and I just bounce back again ...

4

Why it is never too late to learn something new

It is never too late to learn something new, either for pleasure or for profit, but learning as an adult in retirement is very different from learning at school as you may remember it. You now have plenty of choice about what you learn, the speed at which you learn, the way you learn, and when you learn. Moreover, there has never been such a range of opportunities available, whether in the community, over the internet, or by correspondence.

Facing up to the challenge

Does the thought of picking up the cudgels again faze you?

Walk into any continuing education centre or the online section of your local library and you will discover that the bulk of the populace is composed of your peers in retirement. Why do they pick up the cudgels again? They do so because it adds to their quality of life in disparate ways. Most of them would tell you that while they found the prospect daunting to begin with, they soon got into the way of things, because of the helpful assistance always on tap for beginners. Some even progress to become tutors, like Malcolm in 'Case study 5' on page 48.

Do you feel that all this new technology stuff is beyond you?

It is a natural reaction at almost any age to back off when confronted with innovation of which you have no prior experience. However, in three of the case studies featured below, you will read about septuagenarians who refused to be intimidated. They all quickly perceived a purpose in learning how to apply the newfangled technology to their advantage. So will you when you give it a try and come to realise that becoming proficient isn't nearly as difficult as some might have you believe.

Do you doubt that expanding your education will benefit you?

Don't abandon learning as you enter the third age. Take it with you and keep expanding it. The more you learn in retirement the more you will enhance your lifespan, because learning not only stretches the mind but it also refreshes every sinew in the body. It is the stuff of which you are made; it energises the stratosphere, the very air you breathe. In 'Case study 1', you will learn how Joslyn Ross at the age of 76 caught the learning bug and went on to complete six individual courses.

Do you think that studying for a degree is a fanciful notion?

Many retirees go the whole hog and engage in study to bring their education up to graduate level. Would you consider applying for a degree course or do you think that is just a fanciful notion? It never occurred to Margaret MacEwen that it might be regarded as bizarre. She not only applied but also graduated, after which she went off globetrotting. When she returns, as you will read in 'Case study 2', she intends to master Italian. Margaret, incidentally, is in her 90th year.

Do you worry that your studies may prove too costly?

Then fear not, because the majority of the learning facilities listed in this chapter are completely free of charge. Even if you set your heart on a course that does involve some personal cost, you may still qualify for financial assistance.

Do you consider it too late in the day to become involved?

Some retirees shy away from expanding their education and engaging with information technology (IT) under the mistaken impression that mastering the beast will prove too difficult. Nothing could be further from the truth, so get cracking, join in, and add a new dimension to your experience of the third age.

Adult learning in the community

Adult learning is very well established. More than 1 million adults took part in classes in 2003, and there are plenty of opportunities to learn in your own area, for example, at local colleges, community centres, church or village halls, family gathering places, or sports venues. What you can learn is just as varied, so whatever your interest, you should find a course to suit you. You could learn new skills to add zest to your third-age adventure, pick up where you left off in your study of languages at school, or acquire commercial expertise that might tempt you to start a small business.

You will never know if adult learning in the community is for you unless you give it a try, and it is easy to get started. The opportunities are open to everyone and are ideal if you don't want to travel too far. Many of the courses will run over a number of weeks, so if you are willing to commit to going regularly, you should find something on tap to suit you.

You can find out more by contacting such bodies as your local authority, college, or Learning and Skills Council. There are also plenty of voluntary organisations that cater for adult learning needs, such as the Workers' Educational Association and the University of the Third Age (see below).

Case study 1

Joslyn (76) completes six courses

Joslyn Ross is an inspiration for people who want to take up learning late in life, but perhaps don't have the confidence to do so. His appetite for knowledge developed while he was recovering from a fall, in which he hurt his back and ankle. Joslyn had to start his education from scratch, with help from staff at Bilston Community College in Wolverhampton. Since then he has done many courses, including English, maths, photography, IT, desktop publishing, and public speaking.

'It was hard at first,' says Joslyn, 'but I decided that I couldn't continue all my life relying on others to help me. Now I can't stop.'

Case study 2

Margaret (90) is an inspiration to all retirees

This letter from a reader appeared in a national newspaper on Saturday 7 February 2004:

Reading the story of pensioner Margaret MacEwen in your newspaper recently gave me a real boost – it just shows you are never too old to learn. The amazing Margaret, at 90, has become one of Scotland's oldest graduates. As if that wasn't remarkable, now she is off to visit a niece in Australia and when she returns she intends to start learning Italian! Good luck to her, she deserves to be honoured by the Queen.

How about it, Your Royal Highness?

Case study 3

Jack and Sam (over 50) go back to school ...

The extract that follows is from an article by Joanne Waldman, MEd, which was posted on a retirement website (www.retirement-options.com):

Would you have the courage to change your career and go back to school if you were in your early or late 50s? Could you study for and pass a college exam? Both Jack and Sam, in their 50s, chose to make major career changes by becoming teachers, one of high school science, the other of elementary age children. Layoffs and business decline led to thoughts of 'What do I do now with my life?' Jack had worked as a chemist in his first career, and even has a master's degree in chemistry. During his years of employment at one company, Jack took on more and more computer duties and eventually transitioned out of chemistry into IT. Years later he was laid off from another company as the head of the IT department. The idea of teaching never crossed his mind until a friend suggested he apply for a six-week position teaching chemistry. 'Twenty-five years ago I would have laughed at the suggestion of becoming a teacher. The biggest surprise is that I really like teaching.'

How easy is it to make a decision of this magnitude? Sam, who is currently 59 years of age, wishes he had done it ten years sooner. 'I wish someone had blown in my ear the words "you have the ability do this" and maybe I would have considered it earlier.' And what is it like to be in a classroom, learning with students who are 19–21 years of age? Jack is surprised at how well he has been accepted by the younger students. He did have an incident when he taught his first lab as a teaching assistant. One of the students assumed that he was a professor and addressed him as one. Jack was quick to let the student know that he too was a student. Even with the average age of first retirement at 57, neither man foresees retiring in the near future. As with many baby boomers, these men are choosing to continue working. Sam feels that teaching offers him some flexibility and options in later retirement years. For example, if he chooses to relocate, he would be able to get a teaching job in the new location. Jack advises, 'I think that you have to have an open mind at my age to say that I may need to do something else to move forward with my life.'

Jack and Sam exercised their options to keep on working, but in tandem laid down essential foundations for an enriching retirement in future years.

The University of the Third Age

The University of the Third Age (U3A) offers a range of learning opportunities delivered *by older people for older people.* The options include French, IT, music, history, art, and literature.

Is it for me?

The U3A certainly could be for you, now that you are retired and have time in plenty to stretch your innate abilities. The U3A, which has more than 500 local groups in the UK, is for retirees who want to learn in an informal, relaxed atmosphere. Read what one retiree has to say on the matter in 'Case study 4'.

How can I find out more?

Phone 020 7837 8838 or visit www.u3a.org.uk for details of your nearest U3A group.

Case study 4

Pat (55) convenes two U3A groups

'It's a misconception that the University of the Third Age is all about taking high-level exams,' says 55-year-old Pat O'Donnell of Bangor, County Down. 'It's for people who love to learn, but in an informal, friendly environment. I'm now a convenor for two groups, including one on music appreciation. The U3A is great, because if you want to learn about a subject, all you have to do is find some like-minded people and set up your own group.'

Adult e-learning

Learndirect

A prime example of adult e-learning is the government-sponsored learndirect, the largest e-learning network in the UK. Learndirect allows people to study at their local centre or anywhere where they can get access to a computer and the internet.

Is it for me?

Most of the courses are online, so if you don't fancy going back to the classroom or you can't fit a regular session into your schedule, you may feel that this is the option for you. Learning on the internet means that you can learn at a speed to suit you, in a place to suit you, and at any time you like. No one need be fazed by the prospect of engaging in electronic tuition, because guidance for beginners is an integral part of the service.

How can I find out more?

The learndirect national learning advice line offers information and unbiased advice about all areas of learning and leisure. Whether you are interested in computers, local history, or business, or you want to learn to read or write better, you can contact the learndirect national learning advice line. Phone the advice line free on 0800 100 900 (open seven days a week from 9 a.m. to 10 p.m.).

Alternatively, you can visit the national website at www.learndirect.co.uk (Fig. 4.1).

Scotland has its own website at www.learndirect-scotland.com, which is where a 74-year-old Shetlander discovered how easy it is to find one's way through the veritable

Fig. 4.1 The largest e-learning network in the UK

maze of courses on offer: 70,000 in all from learning centres, colleges, universities, and private training providers. The septuagenarian's story is told in 'Case study 6'.

Case study 5

Malcolm (disabled) achieves IT qualifications

Former coal miner Malcolm Pierrepont left school with no qualifications and no desire to get any. But after being out of work for five years, he decided he needed to occupy his time more positively.

'I was always bad at English at school,' says Malcolm, who lives near Barnsley. 'I asked around to see if there was anything close by to help me improve myself, and was put in contact with the local resource centre.'

Since then, Malcolm, who has physical disabilities from a spinal disease, hasn't looked back. Through the resource centre and learndirect, he has achieved several qualifications in computer studies, including spreadsheets, word processing, databases, and desktop publishing. Malcolm was enjoying himself so much that he decided to become a voluntary IT tutor at the resource centre.

'I enjoy teaching people. I was once in their position myself – not knowing much about computers,' he says.

Case study 6

Willie (74) masters computer skills

In a special supplement to the *Daily Record* newspaper of 23 October 2003, Shetland pensioner and grandfather of three Willie Spence recalls that learning how to use a computer became a personal goal that he was determined to achieve.

'I really wanted to learn how to email so that I could stay in touch with my daughters in Edinburgh and Aberdeen. I was ready for a challenge and learning how to use a computer seemed the obvious choice.'

Willie and his wife Christina went to Shetland's Telecroft 2000 Learning Centre.

Says Willie, 'We signed up for an introductory course through flexible learning which meant we could go at our own pace. I was really amazed to see the opportunities that opened up to both of us as a result of learning how to use a computer. Learning something new is good for everyone, regardless of how old you are. I am very proud of my achievements. Whatever your goals and aims may be, learning can help you achieve them.'

This retired RAF foreman progressed from having no computing skills to becoming so adept with the keyboard and mouse that he bought a computer for personal use at home.

UK online centres

Sponsored by the government, UK online centres target those with low or zero IT skills by providing an opportunity for everyone to use computers and access the internet. Approachable and experienced operatives are available to provide as much help as required. The online centres help you get to grips with IT, experience the internet, and gain new skills at your own pace in a supportive and friendly atmosphere.

Are they for me?

If you have never used a computer before, aren't sure about technology, or don't have access to a computer, you will find more than 6000 UK online centres to give you as much help as you need to get started. The online centres are housed in all sorts of places, for example, community centres, churches, schools, and libraries. Some are even mobile. Regrettably, UK online centres are available in England only at present.

How can I find out more?

For your nearest UK online centre, or for more information, you can phone the UK online centres helpline on **0800 77 1234**. The line is open seven days a week from 7 a.m. to 11 p.m. You can also visit www.dfes.gov.uk/ukonlinecentres/ to keep tabs on the inevitable expansion of the scheme throughout the rest of the country.

Case study 7

Lillian (70) traces her husband's ancestry

'I've managed to trace my husband's family tree and helped him to find out what happened to his father, who was killed in action in the war – all thanks to the internet and the team at the UK online centre in Manchester,' says 70-year-old Lillian Galloway.

If you would like to trace your own family history, you might want to read Dianne Marelli's *Meet Your Ancestors* (How To Books, 2003) to get you on the fast track.

The People's Network

The People's Network is another government project, which aims to make sure that every public library in the country is linked to the internet and has sufficient funding for computers. More than 4,000 library centres were up and running by the end of 2002, and specially trained operatives are available to help you learn new skills and find information.

Is it for me?

'People can come here as often as they like to check their emails or sign up for various courses on the PC,' says Julie Jones, Head of Library and Museum Services in Rhondda Cynon Taff. 'We've also teamed up with the local branch of Age Concern to offer the over-50s one-to-one sessions on using email and the internet. Most people had not used a computer before and one man liked it so much he bought one for himself. Others liked it for the social aspect. Not only do people meet other people, they can also email friends and family abroad and keep in touch. They can learn what they wish at their own speed.'

If you want to use computers and get access to the internet, the People's Network can help.

How can I find out more?

Contact your local library, phone 020 7273 1401, or visit www. peoplesnetwork.gov.uk to find out about your nearest centre.

Adult distance learning

Adult distance learning is changing people's lives.

The Learning Library

The Learning Library is an initiative that enables you to study at home, training in your own time at your own pace. You don't require previous experience to participate, and the qualifications you can obtain are nationally recognised. The courses are up to date, clear, and easy to understand, and all books, learning materials, and professional software are supplied. You are even allowed free telephone and postal access to your allocated tutor. Visit www.thelearninglibrary .ac.uk for complete information on how to use the Learning Library to study at home.

You might want to think about starting your own business at home with the aid of one or more of these training courses from the Learning Library.

Programming with Visual Basic.net

Visual Basic is the most widely used programming language in the world. In this course, you will learn to:

o create stand-alone Visual Basic applications.

Manual bookkeeping

In this course, you will cover:

o cash transactions
o credit transactions
o the ledger
o the cash book

o trial balances
o final accounts
o VAT and PAYE
o bank reconciliation
o control accounts
o the journal.

Sage computerised bookkeeping

Sage is the most widely used accounting software application in the world. In this course, you will cover:

o the sales ledger
o the purchase ledger
o cash transactions
o credit transactions
o invoices
o VAT returns
o trial balances
o financial reports
o profit and loss
o balance sheets.

Computer skills with Microsoft Office XP

In this course, you will learn to use:

o Microsoft (word processing)
o Microsoft Excel (spreadsheets)
o Microsoft PowerPoint (graphics)
o clip art
o mailmerge
o templates
o databases
o graphics.

Computer maintenance

In this course, you will learn to:

o build a personal computer (PC) for a fraction of the cost; and

o run a computer maintenance business.

Web design

In this course you will learn to:

o create a personal or business website; and

o get the most out of the internet.

More distance-learning opportunities for adults

You are never too old to learn nowadays and you don't even have to leave home to do so. The internet allows you to study any subject of your choice at a wide range of universities or colleges worldwide.

Education World (www.education-world.com)

Education World is the place where retirees can go to find literally thousands of courses from all over the world on every conceivable subject. If the course you want is at, say, the University of Southern California, then you can sign up for a distance-learning course. The website is superbly detailed and includes a neatly organised listing of links to other schools and universities.

The National Open College Network (www.nocn.org.uk)

The National Open College Network (NOCN) is one of the largest awarding bodies in the UK. Accessibility to education is what it is all about. The website is open to everyone, and a lack of conventional qualifications shouldn't be a barrier. The NOCN operates a national credit framework through 31 local Open College Networks based across the UK, offering just about every course you could dream of.

The Learning Network (www.rgu.ac.uk/abs)

The Learning Network is the online arm of the Open College, which is in turn a sister organisation of the Open University. The website addresses the difficulties of distance learning, and is tailored to suit newcomers to electronic tuition. It is devoted to promoting access to education for as many people as possible and has achieved tremendous success at making distance learning a friendlier and more workable experience.

The National Institute of Adult Continuing Education (www.niace.org.uk)

The National Institute of Adult Continuing Education (NIACE) is the leading non-governmental organisation for adult learning in England and Wales. It aims to give as many adults as possible the opportunity to return to education. With links to more than 2,000 members, it is the place to come for news on what is happening in adult continuing education around the country.

Open University (www3.open.ac.uk/oubs)

The Open University website is another offshoot of the Open University, which is equally good at encouraging adult learning via the internet. It covers management education and pulls on 30 years' experience of the Open University. With more than 25,000 enthusiasts a year studying, this is one of the world's largest business schools.

Third Age (www.thirdage.com)

This refreshing website provides a selection of retiree distance-learning opportunities in a lighter vein: outdoor activities, beauty and style, games, health, horoscopes, money, personals, travel (Fig. 4.2). Membership is free.

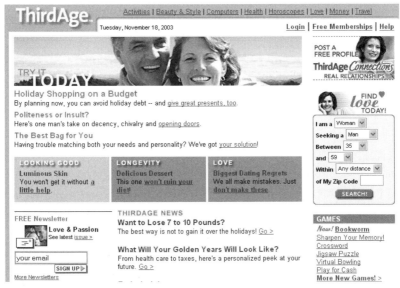

Fig. 4.2 Distance-learning opportunities for retirees

Case study 8

Bob (83) wins the Real Silver Surfer of the Year Award

Adult Learners' Week (12–16 May) is orchestrated by NIACE, and Friday 16 May has become known as Silver Surfers' Day. On that day in 2003, the Real Silver Surfer of the Year Award was won by octogenarian Bob Middlemas.

Bob was born in County Durham in 1920. In 1939 he enlisted in the Royal Marines and after 22 years' service he received an honourable discharge and a long-service pension. His retirement interests include sea and freshwater fishing, gardening, wood-turning, and photography – including developing.

In 1997 Bob started to take an interest in digital photography, but still preferred his Canon camera and darkroom. Then, a year later, he bought his first PC and taught himself the way around. He is now on his third PC, and the Canon film camera is gone, re-placed by a Canon D60 digital camera. The traditional darkroom techniques have also disappeared, having been swapped for Photoshop image manipulation.

Bob still goes online every day, sharing his hobby and ex-pertise with new-found friends around the world. He helped set up the photography studio at www.idf50.co.uk, which in 2002 received a good project award from the EU. Bob's superb creative photography and free advice over the web give pleasure and in-spiration to like-minded enthusiasts all over the world.

Financial help for adult learning

If you locate a course that really interests you but has a hefty price tag attached, don't be put off. Depending on the category of learning (whether the course is provided by your LEA or by an educational institution like a university or a further education college), different kinds of financial help may be available to help you. For example, you may be eligible for reduced fees on LEA courses. Most help is provided at community level, and what you get may be affected by your individual circumstances. Your LEA or local college will be able to offer advice about any financial assistance you may qualify for. The booklet *Money to Learn* (Department for Education and Skills, 2002) provides general information on assistance for all adult learners. You can view the booklet online at www.lifelonglearning.dfes.gov.uk/moneytolearn/ or order a printed copy by emailing dfes@prolog.uk.com or phoning 0845 60 222 60.

What you will gain by participating

Spend a few hours a week in adult learning activities and you will:

o open up new horizons to enrich your retirement;
o create fulfilment rather than just fill in time;
o enhance your innate abilities;
o master new skills;
o come to terms with IT;
o explore the wonder of the internet; and
o discover new hobby interests.

Personal case study

There wasn't nearly as much help around when I ascended the third plateau back in 1994, but I managed somehow. A willing administrator compromised on my age and put me down for an IT course, which got me up to speed in a very short time. Nowadays, the choices are plentiful and in many cases entirely free. Don't be a shy-away: participate in adult learning. I guarantee you won't be disappointed.

5

Why getting up to speed in cyberspace opens up new vistas

There are currently 12.6 million websites devoted exclusively to the subject of retirement, which makes this chapter an important add-on to what you have just read. We are still on the IT learning curve and looking now at alternative routes for getting you up to speed in cyberspace. There is so much you can do to enrich your retirement when you take time out to investigate the possibilities, and it is easy because the internet abounds with free online courses, learning materials, tools, and contrasting third-age interests when you know where to look. If you are new to the wonders of cyberspace, here are a dozen fresh horizons to explore as you get started:

1 surfing the web;
2 understanding email;
3 creating your own website;
4 mastering new skills online;

5 planning holidays online;

6 tracing your ancestry online;

7 locating lost friends online;

8 making new friends online;

9 researching your favourite topics online;

10 finding hobby options online;

11 going window-shopping online; and

12 joining a third-age community online.

Discovering one thing leads you to discover another, and it should never be a chore. You don't even have to own a computer to participate – all you need is your ticket to free public-library online facilities. Even so, you will have questions about exploring fresh horizons online, so let us try to anticipate a few.

Isn't surfing the web just for kids?

Not so, according to official research findings. A recent Forrester Survey (the internet's research arm) reveals that 32.7 per cent of all regular web users are over 60 years of age. This startling statistic can be evidenced by visiting any public-library online section, where there is always a goodly sprinkling of grey hairs among the students cramming and the kids hammering the game consoles. Third-age people are swarming in droves to the internet and using it for entertainment, education, and enlightenment. Couldn't you benefit from joining your peers and surfing the web to open up new vistas?

Isn't it a bit late to be dabbling with email?

It is never too late to get up to date. Coming to terms with email is almost a priority nowadays. Email is the fast, easy, modern way to keep in touch with friends, children, grand-children, and, for some of us, great-grandchildren. It is simple to operate, saves on time, and needn't ever cost you a penny. There are hundreds of free online providers with whom you can subscribe, obtain your own email address, and access tuition if required. My personal favourite is www.hotmail.com because of its range of ancillary services, most of which are especially useful for active retirees.

What would I do with a website?

Just a few years ago, if you were not acquainted with hyper text mark-up language (HTML), you would have struggled to build a website. Not so nowadays with the advent of point-and-click electronic tools. They make website creation as simple as building a structure with Lego blocks. So what could you do with your own website? You could treat it as a project to:

o chart your own achievements and those of your family;
o trace your ancestry;
o start a business in retirement (see also Chapter 7);
o impart your accumulated knowledge to others (see also Chapter 9); and
o develop a hobby interest (see also Chapter 10).

Why not give it a go using a free service such as www.freeservers.com to begin with? Once you get a taste for website creation, you might want to move on to building a second, third, or even fourth website like the 78-year-old webmaster featured in Chapter 10.

How much does it cost to master new skills online?

In truth, it needn't cost you a penny. Start off your search with www.coursepal.com, an extraordinary free website tool that allows you to access syllabuses of third-age interest courses in every conceivable category from worldwide universities and further education colleges (Fig. 5.1).

Registration will cost you nothing, as will right of entry to the majority of the comprehensive tutorials listed at this website. Moreover, complementing the public-sector options we have already covered, the aptly named website www.free-ed.net opens the doors to starting places for alternative free education on the internet: no books to buy, no hidden fees,

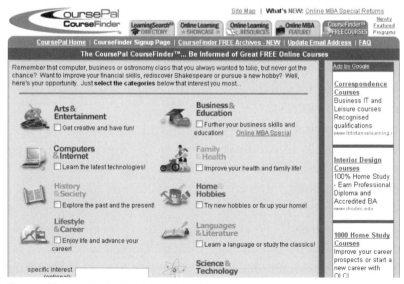

Fig. 5.1 Where to look online for further education courses

and complete tutorials for more than 120 disparate vocational and academic disciplines, including:

o accounting and bookkeeping
o business
o economics
o finance
o marketing and sales
o personal finance
o administration and leadership
o early childhood education
o educational methods
o anthropology
o history
o human ecology
o psychology
o sociology
o art
o English
o English as a second language
o journalism
o modern languages
o classical languages
o performing arts
o literature
o astronomy
o biology
o chemistry
o geography
o earth sciences
o physics
o civil and construction engineering
o industrial engineering

o mechanical engineering
o clinical diagnosis and treatment
o anatomy and physiology
o pharmacy and pharmacology
o computer information systems
o computer languages and scripts
o core mathematics.

Why plan holidays online?

When you use the internet to plan a holiday, you provide yourself with a valuable edge: the option to conclude the deal online or offline as you prefer. Employing the web as a research tool, you eliminate the one-to-one interface in gathering background data for every imaginable type of holiday, from pitching a tent in Cumbria to luxuriating on a Caribbean cruise liner. Wherever your proclivities lie, you need to have access to resources to get the best out of travel in retirement. You need an entrée that lets you in on all you need to know in advance of commitment. Chapter 12 presents you with an all-in-one holiday guide, containing a compendium of links for online planning, which will be of equal value if you decide to effect buying decisions offline.

Wouldn't it prove difficult to trace my ancestry online?

Tracing your ancestry makes for a highly interesting and fulfilling retirement project, one that isn't at all difficult if you go about your research in the correct manner. Very simply, the rule is to begin with the information that you know for certain to be accurate and, using this as a basis of fact, trace backwards in time. Starting with your own birth certificate, you can locate the full names of parents, their ages, and where they lived at the time you were born. With that information alone, you are off to a great start.

Draw up a family tree of your relatives as far back as you know. This helps to give you a clear idea of what you still need to find out and whom you need to contact to find this out. Now you can go online to complete the job. You have many options, but you may wish to visit www.familyfinding.co.uk, a website that provides low-cost tracing of blood relatives. To keep your records, you will either need a folder, a large notebook, or suitable computer software. Personal Ancestry File version 5 is recommended. Visit www.familysearch.org and download it for free.

How do I go about locating lost friends online?

Sometimes you can strike lucky by using a search engine facility. Employing this basic approach I managed to trace a friend I hadn't heard from in over 30 years, but that was only because he had established a minor claim to fame (his name came in at no. 53 on a list of over 13,000 entries). Your best bet is to invest a few pounds in registering at a website that specialises in locating lost friends. Websites such as www.friends-reunited.com and www.ukig.co.uk are among the most highly rated.

How do I make new friends online?

Register for free at one of the third-age communities listed a little further on in this chapter. You will discover several alternatives for striking up new friendships. The best way to start is by joining a discussion forum. You could also post a message on the bulletin board, but be very careful how you approach this option. You don't want to invite a potential voyeur to enter your life.

How do I research my favourite topics online?

Conduct an online search for newsgroups that focus on your particular area of interest. No matter how outlandish the topic, you can be assured that will be many other people who share your passion and are only too willing to share research, published articles, and theses on the prescribed subject matter. Couple this tactic with a separate search on www.google.com using appropriate keywords.

Where do I look to find hobby options?

Use a recognised retirees' search facility (see below). Type in a key phrase such as 'retirement hobbies', and away you go. You will be presented with hundreds of useful options. You might also visit the portal website www.retirement-matters.co.uk (Fig. 5.2), which has links to 35 hobby interest websites, including antiques, art, bridge, chess, crochet, dancing, museums, and writing, among others. Add these to the list of more than 50 retirement hobbies discussed in Chapter 10.

Why go window-shopping online?

Cast your mind back 20 years or so to the prototypes of today's out-of-town electronic superstores. In the main they were cold uninviting sheds stuffed with cardboard boxes containing branded merchandise. Before you would consider making a purchase at one of these barren outlets, you would invariably visit your local high-street electricity showroom to compare prices and (equally important) obtain the vital prod-

Fig. 5.2 A UK retirement portal

uct knowledge that was rarely forthcoming at the discount stores. Then, if price was the prime consideration, you would hand over your cash at one of the sheds and collect your box at the counter.

Online window-shopping is the modern equivalent of this scenario, except that it eliminates trolling around stores and presents you with everything on tap – price comparisons and specifications from all the major chains – so enabling you to make a value judgement as to whether you buy online or offline (and online is a temptation because of the pounds clipped off to boost web sales).

Why join a third-age community online?

There are available to you, free of charge, several exclusive senior citizens' portals that lead to a myriad of resources to enhance the third-age years. They aren't to everyone's liking, and there is only one way to establish whether participation in one of these communities might suit you: investigate the possibilities.

Let us review the benefits accruing when you register your interest at these remarkable cyberspace portals. Then, we will round matters off with the web addresses of three portals worthy of exploration. The first portal (Wired Seniors) provides an international network of links, while the other two portals (Retirement Matters and 50Connect) give links to UK websites. In essence what they all provide is a one-stop resource for active retirees with features such as these.

o **Retirees' search facilities:** These aren't ordinary search engines; the emphasis is on third-age projects designed exclusively for the over-50s.

o **Discussion forums:** Jump right in and start a discussion on any topic you like: government, politics, the weather, health concerns, social security issues, whatever. You name it, and someone will be interested in your views. Of course they may not agree with them, but they will be interested enough to post a reply. In no time at all you will have a lively, healthy discussion going with seniors from around the world. Discussion forums are the place to share ideas, opinions, and friendship with other members.

o **Bulletin boards:** Messages posted are divided into categories to make them easier to browse. If you prefer, you may also search through the aggregated communications using the keyword option tool.

o **Retirees' radio:** The radio service www.wiredseniors. com is a vital part of the network that makes up the Wired Seniors portal. It offers an extensive variety of retirement-oriented information and programming. To listen in, you will need a player loaded up to your computer. That isn't a problem, because you can download the appropriate software for free at the website. The player software does all the work of taking the audio and video from the web and translating it into a format that you can hear and watch on your computer.

o **Retirees' discount malls:** All of these malls have special price deals for seniors, or in some cases, offer special services for retirees. Merchants from around the world are featured. Browse around to see what they have to offer.

o **Retirees helping retirees:** Third-age people have a great deal of experience and knowledge to contribute to society. Perhaps visitors can help you, or you can help others, by answering questions that you or they may have in categories such as these:

   o computer hardware
   o computer software
   o cooking
   o gardening
   o home maintenance
   o internet
   o pets
   o photography
   o sports
   o trivia.

o **Scam reports:** Retirees are a favourite target of scam operators. The Wired Seniors portal emails special scam bulletins to members from time to time, as well as posting some of the more common rip-offs on the portal website.

Wired Seniors (www.wiredseniors.com)

The Wired Seniors portal is the central hub of many international websites relating to seniors (Fig. 5.3).

It is the global gateway to a wide variety of retirement-oriented information and resources.

Retirement Matters (www.retirement-matters.co.uk)

The Retirement Matters portal comprises ten UK websites covering:

1 UK, overseas, and specialist travel
2 finance, pensions, and annuities
3 news headlines; special offers
4 penfriends, genealogy, reunions, and friends
5 an eyecare, health, and GP forum
6 care services, mobility, hearing, and charities
7 motoring and online shopping
8 leisure, hobbies, entertainment, sports, and pets
9 home and garden; retirement homes
10 advertisements.

Fig. 5.3 A worldwide retirement portal

50Connect (www.50connect.co.uk)

The UK-based portal 50Connect focuses on a multifaceted selection of retirement topics housed in 25 individual 'channels'.

Wiring up for the third age has practical advantages

We need all the help we can muster in our quest for fulfilment in retirement. Getting wired up in cyberspace assumes increasing importance as you dig more deeply into its potential: entering one avenue prompts you to scrutinise another. Only recently in my web wanderings, I stumbled across something to my personal advantage – the website www.vet eransagency.mod.uk – which may also be of interest to those of you who, like me, are veterans the armed forces (I served with the RAF during the Korean conflict). The website contains lots of interesting information for retirees. Among the fact-packed pages, I recently discovered that veterans may be eligible for assistance with energy savings. Grants (sometimes covering all costs) are available for retirees receiving war pensions and other benefits. These grants may apply to a range of products from cavity-wall and loft insulation to central-heating systems. Upon further investigation, I also determined that *even if you aren't a veteran*, you may find it worth your while to contact the following to find out what additional help is available offline.

o **Warm Front:** Phone 0800 952 0600.
o **Your local authority/council:** Check your local phone book for contact details.

o **Energy Savings Trust:** Phone 0800 512 012.

o **Energy companies:** Contact numbers will be displayed on your gas or electricity bills. You can also contact other energy suppliers to establish what help they can provide.

o **Staywarm:** Phone 0800 1 694 694. Staywarm has a scheme designed for the over-60s, and it works like this. However much gas or electricity you need, you pay a fixed low price – weekly, fortnightly, or monthly. The amount you pay is based on the number of people who live in your home and the number of bedrooms it contains.

Get wired up in cyberspace and add flavour to your retirement with the practical advantages you will gain. Don't be put off if you don't have a computer connected to the internet. Use the free services we have already identified.

6

Why keeping your hand in part-time can prove beneficial

It is perfectly understandable that many of us experience a numbing void when we retire from day-to-day involvement in the career that occupied the bulk of our time. The experience can prove doubly unnerving when there is no plan for replacement in position. Don't let this happen to you. Expanding your education won't keep you fully occupied, so in order to enjoy a fulfilling third age, you would do well to consider stretching your abilities further in one or more of the part-time work options featured in this chapter and elsewhere in the book.

Let us kick off with some questions you might want to ask yourself about becoming involved in part-time work.

o Am I sufficiently fit to do part-time work?
o Will part-time work help to fill a gap in my new lifestyle?
o Will part-time work affect my state pension?
o What about deductions like National Insurance?

o Do I need the extra cash that part-time work will bring in?

o Do I go back to what I worked at before?

o Do I look at something entirely different?

o Do I possess special skills I have never tested out in the workplace?

o Where do I look for opportunities?

Deciding about your fitness

Only you can decide whether you are sufficiently fit to do part-time work. If you are hale and hearty, then you don't have a problem, but if you have even a niggling suspicion about your fitness, then think twice before you take on part-time work. The very last thing you need on entry into the third age is pressure, whether physical, mental, or emotional.

Eliminating the numbing void

Entering retirement necessitates making adjustments to your lifestyle. Among these is a need to find a means of easing the emptiness that is sometimes felt on leaving the workplace, when there is a loss of daily structure, involvement with other people, income, intellectual challenges, and feelings of self-worth and accomplishment. If the sense of emptiness weighs heavily on you, consider whether part-time work might be the answer. Look upon it as a temporary way out of initial uneasiness, so that if it doesn't work out to your satisfaction, you can move on to something else. First, though, read on and equip yourself to make an action plan.

Working after the official retirement age

As you can continue to work after the official retirement age and still pick up your pension, you may find that keeping your hand in part-time is a sensible option. Perhaps though, the thought of returning to the workplace that accounted for 30, 40, or 50 years of your life is anathema to you, even if it wasn't for the luminaries quoted in the opening chapter. Should this be the case, then undertake some research on making a fresh start in part-time work.

Gaining exemption from National Insurance contributions

Should you proceed to take up part-time work, here is something you must do without delay: obtain a certificate of exemption from National Insurance contributions. If you fail to do so before you start working again, your employer will make unnecessary deductions that you may find difficult to reclaim. While the Contributions Agency will happily provide you with a pre-dated certificate of exemption, they will look to your employer to make recompense – and the employer will almost certainly refer you back to the Contributions Agency for a solution. You will be consistently out of pocket, and it could be some considerable time before matters are rectified. Avoid this unpleasantness by drawing down the appropriate application form at www.inlandrevenue.gov.uk/ nic/ or by writing in advance to:

Inland Revenue
National Insurance Contributions Agency
Benton Park View
Newcastle-upon-Tyne NE98 1ZZ

Accumulating capital from part-time work

For many retirees, the extra cash from part-time work comes in handy for supplementing day-to-day living expenses; for some retirees, the extra cash is more of a necessity. If you are in the fortunate position of not requiring a top-up on your retirement income, but nevertheless consider that part-time work would prove therapeutic, press on with your due diligence. You could always save the income and accumulate some capital to put towards an annuity or the purchase of something or other that would enrich your third-age experience.

Deciding what you would like to work at

Where to start? Right here, right now, with *you*. Is there some project or other that you often felt a yen to pursue but never got around to, because of the anxiety that would follow from leaving behind (if such a thing still exists) a secure occupation? Is there a special skill you have, which for the same reason has never been put to the test in an employment scenario? Such pressures no longer exist, so think about what you would *like* to work at before arriving at a decision.

Projecting your abilities in a new direction

Not everyone is lucky enough to spend a lifetime working in a job that fulfilled all their expectations and stretched their innate abilities to the utmost. It might have appeared like a satisfactory occupation to other people, but not to the person walking the walk. Should this description fit you, perhaps you might think about projecting your abilities in a new direction on a part-time basis. Let me illustrate this proposition with a real-life example. Among my circle of acquaintances is a recent retiree whose career revolved around the sharp end of international marketing. He was good at his job, travelled the world, and made a lot of money, but he frequently confided in me that he couldn't wait to shed his image. He just *didn't like* what he did for a living. When he retired, much to the consternation of his family, he took up a part-time position with a garden landscape concern – and he loves what he is now doing.

Putting special skills to the test

In much the same category, maybe you retired from a career that never once provided an opportunity to exercise a special skill you possess. Could you find a part-time opening in retirement to demonstrate your prowess?

Looking for opportunities

Weigh up the pros and cons of going back to work part-time. If you give yourself the green light, decide on the hours, check out your tax situation, obtain a certificate of exemption from National Insurance contributions, search for an opening to your liking, and go for it!

To assist in your deliberations, the government provides two excellent initiatives.

Take a trip on the Worktrain

The Worktrain website (www.worktrain.gov.uk) is designed primarily for those seeking full-time employment but, among the hundreds of opportunity searches available, you will find many temporary and part-time openings (Fig. 6.1).

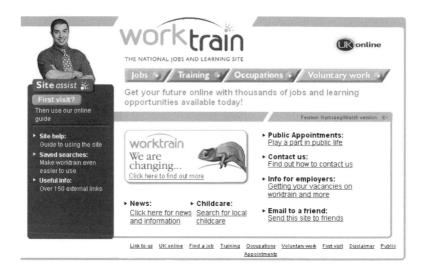

Fig. 6.1 Where to look online for part-time work opportunities

Here is a list of some of the categories you can investigate by going online, choosing any of significance to your particular leanings, and undertaking an exhaustive search for thirty minutes or so.

Central and local government

o civil servants
o administrative and clerical staff.

Financial

o accounts and wages staff
o counter clerks
o credit controllers
o estimators and assessors
o investment analysts
o accounting technicians
o importers and exporters

- o insurance underwriters
- o management accountants
- o pensions and insurance staff
- o taxation experts.

Clerical and administrative

- o general office staff
- o communication officers
- o filing and records staff
- o library assistants
- o research interviewers
- o receptionists
- o stock-control clerks
- o telephonists
- o typists.

Secretarial

- o company secretaries
- o legal secretaries
- o medical secretaries
- o personal assistants.

Arts

- o actors and entertainers
- o artists
- o arts officers
- o producers and directors
- o authors
- o dancers
- o choreographers
- o musicians.

Design and printing

o bookbinders
o print finishers
o graphic designers
o originators
o compositors
o print preparers
o printers
o machine minders
o screen printers.

Textile trades

o clothing cutters
o tanners
o sewing machinists
o tailors and dressmakers
o process operators
o upholsterers
o weavers and knitters.

Crafts

o florists
o furniture makers
o woodworkers
o glass-blowers
o ceramicists
o goldsmiths and silversmiths
o musical instrument tuners.

Media

o advertisers
o public-relations managers
o broadcasters

o journalists
o photographers
o equipment operators.

Bars, hotels, and catering

o bakers
o bartenders
o butchers
o meat cutters
o chefs
o fishmongers
o poultry assistants
o food and drink processors
o hotel porters
o housekeepers
o kitchen assistants
o waiters and waitresses.

Sports

o fitness instructors
o leisure managers
o theme-park assistants
o coach drivers.

Tourism

o flight staff
o rail staff
o tour guides
o travel-agency managers.

Carers

o care workers
o childminders

o nursery nurses

o playgroup leaders.

Health

o ambulance staff

o dental nurses

o dental technicians

o hospital porters

o nursing auxiliaries.

Education

o further education teachers

o schoolteachers

o classroom assistants

o industrial trainers

o nursery teachers.

Motor trades

o motor mechanics

o fitters

o vehicle repairers

o spray painters

o garage attendants and cashiers.

Skilled manufacturing

o operators

o plate workers

o shipwrights

o welders

o pattern makers

o pipe fitters

o sheet-metal workers

o toolmakers.

Skilled trades

o bricklayers and masons
o carpenters and joiners
o electricians
o electrical fitters
o floorers and tilers
o glaziers
o plumbers
o heating engineers
o painters and decorators
o plasterers.

Technicians

o civil engineers
o draughtspeople
o building inspectors.

Horticulture

o gardeners
o grounds assistants.

Customer services

o call-centre staff
o customer-care assistants.

Retail

o cashiers
o checkout operators
o shop assistants
o shelf-fillers.

Warehousing

o storage assistants

o transport and distribution clerks.

Sales and purchasing

o marketing assistants

o purchasing assistants

o sales representatives

o telesales staff.

Cleaning services

o caretakers

o cleaners and domestics

o industrial cleaners

o laundry assistants.

Benefit from New Deal 50 plus

The second government initiative for jobseekers is New Deal 50 plus. As a pensioner, you can still benefit from this initiative. New Deal 50 plus is a voluntary service available through jobcentres and Jobcentre Plus offices. It can help you find the right part-time job through one-to-one advice and financial support. You can gain:

o one-to-one support from a New Deal personal adviser;

o a tax-free weekly wages top-up of up to £40 for part-time work or up to £60 for self-employment, if you have an annual income of £15,000 or less (the wages top-up lasts for up to a year and is paid as part of the Working Tax Credit);

o in-work training grants of up to £1500; and

o access to a discretionary fund to help you with clothes or fares for interviews.

To find out more, phone the New Deal helpline on 0845 606 2626 or the New Deal textphone on 0845 606 0680 (calls charged at a local rate), or contact your local jobcentre or Jobcentre Plus office.

Case study 1

Frank (70) is still up on the roof

Grandfather Frank Brown has been described as the oldest roofer in the UK. At 70 years of age, his legendary skills mean he is still in demand all over the world – from Africa to Hong Kong and South Korea. Despite terminating involvement with his own firm Brown's Roofing Service when he was 65, he has continued to work, proving it is ability and not age that counts.

'I believe that if you are still capable of doing a job, then your age shouldn't come into it,' asserts the 70-year-old roofer.

Too right, Frank.

Case study 2

Keith (over 50) updates his skills

'As well as getting advice and support, the New Deal 50 plus gave my wife and I a regular income of £60 a week, and the opportunity to go on a number of courses,' says Keith Buttery.

Keith made a career change in his 50s to become a self-employed computer trainer, by using his training grant to gain teaching qualifications and the European Computer Driving Licence accreditation.

'There just wasn't anything around ... I had been in the textiles industry since I left school, and if I can successfully retrain, then anyone can.'

Case study 3

John (over 50) finds work as a bartender

Thanks to one-to-one support at his local jobcentre, which included guidance on how to write a CV, John Smith found work at a rugby club where, by helping to run the bar, he tripled the takings.

'It wasn't a case of being told what to do. I gave my mentor my ideas, and she went through them and advised me on whether she thought they were worth pursuing. It was only afterwards I realised I'd been guided into making the best decision.'

Case study 4

John (52) starts his own business

John Roster had been unemployed for 30 months before he found work as a self-employed interior designer, thanks to New Deal 50 plus. His personal adviser helped John to build his confidence and claim the New Deal 50 plus Employment Credit while he got his business off the ground. At his adviser's suggestion, John also used funding from the Adviser Discretion Fund to place a 10-week advertisement for his business in a local newspaper. He received three phone calls in the first two weeks, which finally convinced him that he could survive without benefit.

'And in January 2002, I was able to use the New Deal 50 plus training grant to access training, which will lead to me qualifying as a professional designer,' says 52-year-old John. 'I'm extremely happy to be working again.'

Personal case study

At the outset of my retirement and at a time when I was uncertain as to where my future direction lay, I engaged in several different part-time projects. Although I had spent most of my working life running the show and had reservations about being told what to do, I nevertheless enjoyed a measure of satisfaction from the exercise. My first assignment entailed nationwide merchandising for a well-known range of dehumidifiers, followed immediately thereafter by a stint as a researcher for Paypoint, the one-stop electronic retail device for settling utility accounts. Finally, I spent 18 months as a part time regional sales manager for a national transport concern. Give some thought to part-time work, if only as a stopgap measure as it was for me.

7

Why many retirees opt to start a business for fun or profit

Deciding to become a third-age entrepreneur isn't only a rewarding and self-fulfilling experience; it is also tremendous *fun*, whether you do it for pleasure or profit. Maybe in the past you thought about starting your own business, but wavered because the risks were too great, the timing not right, the economy too bad. This time it is different, because your existence won't depend on success or failure; this time, if you go ahead, you will be treating it as an exercise to add flavour and variety to your retirement.

The purpose of this chapter is to help you determine whether you have what it takes to strike out on your own belatedly and stamp your personality on an enterprise of your very own making. What makes a successful entrepreneur? Having a great idea, being highly creative, having lots of enthusiasm for sure, but are entrepreneurs born or made? If you believe the old saying that 'genius is 1 per cent inspiration and 99 per cent perspiration', you will know that most success is down to hard work. So how do you channel your ideas, creativity, and energy into building your own business in retirement without bursting a blood vessel? Read on ...

Crucial questions to ask yourself before you decide

It is a big decision and one that you should not take lightly. You should be certain in your own mind that this is what you want to undertake as a retirement project. It will take more than a good product or service, and hard work alone won't always be enough. Perhaps most importantly, *are you willing to learn?* You should not expect to know everything from the start, and you won't get everything right. But providing you can measure up to the essential requirements for third-age entrepreneurship, learn from your mistakes, recognise your weaknesses, and capitalise on your strengths, you will find success that much easier to come by.

Ask yourself the questions below. Then, rate yourself as an embryo third-age entrepreneur. If, on balance, you feel you have what it takes to succeed, then go for it ...

1 Are you committed to running a business in retirement?

Personal commitment is germane to success and calls for a certain discipline. Now that you are retired, you have time on your hands to pursue leisure interests that you only ever dreamed about when you were working: time to take a holiday whenever you want, to visit the grandchildren on the spur of the moment. Do you really want to impinge on this free time by contracting to display the dedication that running your own business will entail? Or is your disposition such that you can comfortably couple freedom and commitment with equal dexterity?

2 Are you capable of making decisions on your own?

You can listen to advice from other people, of course, but when it comes to making crucial commercial decisions affecting your own business, you will be out there on your own. Does the prospect faze you, or are you capable of taking it all in your stride?

3 Can you plan ahead for all eventualities?

Success comes sooner when you develop the practice of creating individual strategies for every eventuality: good times, bad times, in-between times. How do you rate yourself at planning ahead? Does it come easily to you, or is it something you will need to work at?

4 Do you get on well with people?

You may be the most personable person you know, but how does your personality stack up in commercial terms? You will be dealing with people on a regular basis at both ends of the spectrum: staff and customers. Can you be objective yet affable in your dealings? Can you learn to put self-interest on the back burner when required?

5 Is your spouse or partner behind you and your decision?

Having the unconditional support of your significant other is essential if you are to make a success of running a business in retirement. Will they feel left out or play an active part in the endeavour? Will there be arguments or agreement over finances? On the other hand, if like me you are now alone in your third-age journey, you may quickly discover that entrepreneurship compensates in part for the loss of a partner.

6 Can you afford to invest in yourself?

Perhaps for the first time ever you are facing up to the prospect of investing not in tangibles such as a home or car, but in *yourself.* Can you afford to make such an investment at this time in your life? Even if you can afford it comfortably, do you really want to invest in yourself (no matter how modest the required investment), or would you rather keep the money in the bank? As with most things in life, you have choices, but only you can decide what is best for you.

7 Can you handle unexpected setbacks?

What happens when you meet the odd inevitable setback? Will you wonder what on earth you have let yourself in for, at what should be a less stressful time of your life? Conversely, do you possess the steeliness to convert apparent stumbling blocks into opportunities? Do you have the grit and enthusiasm to persevere and overcome in temporary adversity?

8 Do you understand the financial side of running a business?

If you were an employee during your working life, do you really have a thorough enough understanding of the financial side of running your own business? To bring yourself up to speed, are you prepared to take advantage of the abundance of free tuition that exists on acquiring commercial nous?

9 Are you ready to consider and make the most of change?

Your entry into the third age is a major change in its own right. Are you ready to consider the implications of adding to your altered circumstances by starting a business in retirement to make the most of change? Does taking this route cause you anxiety, or are you confident about turning the transformation to your advantage?

10 Do you have expertise that will set your business apart?

If so, consider yourself fortunate. Skills that are rare are always in demand and constitute the linchpin of a successful enterprise.

Sources of assistance on initial planning

If your objective is the profit motive as opposed to fun, you will need to get help with the initial planning. While you have several options at your disposal, I would recommend at this early stage that you start by contacting your local branch of a mainstream bank that specialises in small business development. Arrange an informal interview with the appropriate executive, outline your personal aims, and give an indication of your current level of commercial expertise; then close this exploratory discussion by requesting their literature pack focusing on start-up support. Undertake this exercise *before* you settle on an idea for your retirement enterprise. It will give you a feel for what lies ahead, should you decide to proceed.

If on the other hand you consider that it is still early days, and too soon for a one-to-one dialogue, visit www.clearly business.com (a Barclays Bank online initiative), where you will find reams of valuable free information on managing your accounts, controlling cash flow, raising start-up finance, and much more besides. While you are there, you can also order a copy of 'Starting and Running Your Own Business', which will be delivered to your door within days. This comprehensive information wallet will provide you with a thorough grounding on the basics of planning an enterprise.

Finding ideas for a business

Start with yourself: where you are, where you have been, and where you would like to be. Here are a few suggestions to get you started.

Do you have a hobby that you can transform into a business?

Many retirees discover the inspiration for starting a business in the leisure pursuits that have provided interest and stimulation over the years. Let us look at some practical possibilities.

o Perhaps you enjoy dressmaking and have a talent for design and the creation of exclusive patterns. Is there a market in your locality for producing made-to-measure garments for busy women who just don't have the time to shop?

o Does your hobby interest revolve around making and arranging flowers? If so, you might consider cashing in on the growing trend of servicing local retail outlets: plants for the exterior, floral arrangements for indoors.

o Do you have nimble fingers and a flair for macramé, mosaic art, or both? With a little string, you can make belts or key rings; with a lot of string, you can make planters or wall hangings, threaded with tiny pieces of glass, stone, clay, or seed to create imaginative designs. These are ancient arts that are once again thriving. Could you supply local market traders? Ask around and show samples of your work.

o If your passion is for woodwork, you might decide to specialise in a particular item or items of furniture, or offer to build fittings to customers' own specifications.

Can you transform your former work into a business?

Not everyone wants to return to the scene of the workplace, but for some it provides the launch pad for a third-age enterprise of their own creation. If you enjoyed what you did for a living, you might derive some inspiration from these factual examples.

o Retired carpet fitters frequently set up in business to service retailers and consumers alike; the retailer saves on labour costs and the consumer on price.

o Service technicians in consumer electronics often create a steady retirement income stream by offering a repair and maintenance service to both traders and the general public.

o Retired advertising executives regularly set themselves up as catalysts for matching clients with, and introducing business to, advertising agencies.

o Retired book editors commonly venture into editorial consultancy, assessing scripts and advising would-be authors.

Are other retirees running businesses that inspire you?

Look around at what other retirees are getting up to in the

way of running part-time businesses. You will find that some of them are involved in:

o answering services
o antique dealership
o bed and breakfast
o building
o catering
o consultancy
o day care
o desktop publishing
o floristry
o garage sales
o garden maintenance
o home handyman services
o import and export services
o image-making
o information services
o insurance broking
o interior design
o online auctions
o painting and decorating
o photography
o plumbing
o sundry online ventures.

Several of the small businesses listed here make ideal third-age ventures, because they offer flexibility in terms of how much commitment you want to make, and for most of them you can use your own home as the base. Let us look at a few examples.

Bed and breakfast

I have a retired friend in Colchester who runs a thriving bed and breakfast. He is now in his early 70s and, like me, widowed. As he owns his property, including all goods and chattels, his running costs are minimal. Apart from food, his only operating expense is the hire of a part-time cook, who also waits tables and does the housekeeping. His own involvement is minimal, allowing him plenty of free time to pursue other retirement interests. Why did he choose to run a bed and breakfast? Because he had occasion to stay in many during his working life, and reckoned he could do a better job than most of the establishments he visited.

Consultancy

If you were fortunate enough in your career to acquire skills that are always in demand, you would do well to consider setting up as a part-time consultant when you retire. Expertise is at a premium in all walks of industry and commerce, and isn't always available for full-time engagement. Start-up costs are minimal, operating expenses next to nothing, and you can commit to as much or as little time on the venture as you please. Calling on old contacts to begin with, you can gradually build up an income-generating clientele who will value the wisdom that accompanies greying hair.

Garden maintenance

If you really enjoy tending your own garden, then why not try garden maintenance as a retirement venture? You can choose how many hours a week you want to work and you need virtually no capital outlay to start (you have probably already got most of the tools you will need). As more and more households now have both partners out working all day, with little or no leisure time, you won't have any problem finding customers. Add to that those people to whom gardening is an abomination. They all need your services. Moreover, if garden design and planning happen to be your forte, there are increasing numbers of newbuild homes that will welcome your expertise.

Home handyman services

If you were a tradesman or have always been handy around the house, you could set yourself up to perform handyman services for those who can't do it themselves or don't have the time. Make it clear what you do and that you expect to get paid for your time – don't just fix things for free. Save your customers money and build up a nice little income stream in your retirement years. If you already have the tools, you won't need to invest anything and you can allocate your time according to your other interests. I have a brother-in-law (a retired colonel in the Royal Canadian Air Force) who runs his own home handyman business. He loves it, and reckons he has found his true calling at last!

Evaluating and testing your business ideas

Here are some questions to help clarify your thoughts about a specific business you may have in mind.

o Is the proposed business something I will enjoy doing? (Think about what your favourite activities are and what you like to do by way of service to other people.)
o Does the business serve an expanding need for which there is no close substitute?
o Can I be so good at a specialised, targeted need that customers will think there is no close substitute?
o Can I handle the capital requirements?

o Can I learn the business by working for someone else first?

o Can I operate as a 'hollow' operation (that is, an operation in which many jobs, such as manufacturing and packaging, are outsourced), without a factory and with a minimum number of employees?

o Is the business product or service one that I can test first?

o Do I consider a partner who has complementary skills to mine or who can help finance the business?

Fine-tuning the evaluation process

At the top of a blank sheet of paper, write the name of an activity you would like to pursue. (If there are several options and you haven't yet made up your mind, create a separate sheet for each alternative.) List all the businesses you can think of that are related to the activity, and then list all the relevant products or services. Use your imagination and jot down every conceivable contender. Refine the list to those businesses that do better in bad times (one may be appropriate for you).

For the purposes of illustration, let us hone the runners even further to just three examples from the list featured above in 'Finding ideas for a business': bed and breakfast, home handyman services, and garden maintenance. You can now make a comparative evaluation using the checklist in Table 7.1, or better still your own checklist. Rank the business ideas on a scale of 1 to 10, with 1 being the lowest and 10 the highest, as in Table 7.1. This kind of analysis can help you gain objectivity in selecting your business.

Once you have decided what business you want to start, try doing the following.

Table 7.1 Checklist for evaluating your business ideas

Objective	Bed and breakfast	Home handy- man services	Garden maintenance
Can I do what I love to do?	6	3	10
Can I fill an expanding need?	5	8	10
Can I specialise?	7	8	10
Can I learn and test the business first, without major investment?	9	8	9

1 Construct a for-and-against list regarding characteristics of the business. On a blank piece of paper, draw a vertical line down the middle of the page, and annotate on one side all the pluses and on the other all the minuses. Sometimes this technique can help to clarify your thinking.

2 Then write down the names of at least five successful businesses in your chosen field. Analyse what these concerns have in common and list the reasons that make them successful.

3 Talk to several people in your intended business. Don't be afraid of the negative aspects. Instead, seek out the pitfalls: better to confront them now than after you open your doors.

4 Write down the information you glean.

5 Observe the competition that isn't doing well and analyse the reasons.

Learning the ropes

Before you even start to think about running a business, start thinking about how to become completely qualified.

o The best way to become qualified is to go to work for someone in the same business – even if only for a few weeks.

o Attend all the classes you can on the subjects you need, for example, accounting, technology, and selling.

o Read all the appropriate how-to books you can locate.

o Don't be afraid to ask questions or seek help from the most successful people in your intended business.

Test-marketing a particular idea

You now need to consider whether there is a quantifiable demand for your product or service. The best way to establish that is to dip your toe in the water with some basic test-marketing. For example, you want to set up in business using your work skills to get two bites at the cherry, like the retired carpet fitters and service technicians mentioned earlier. Here is what you do.

1 Create an outline for your idea.

2 Select your catchment area of operation, highlight the traders you wish to service, and draw up a list of the residential areas where you think your direct customer base lives.

3 Bounce your idea off your local public-sector small business advisory initiative. (The initiative will go under different names according to where you live. Check your local phone book or ask your local council for more information.) Armed with a well-reasoned outline, you should not find it difficult to persuade the advisory body to cover the printing costs of a small run of two-colour flyers.

4 Produce your flyer, mail it to the traders, and deliver it by hand in the residential areas.

5 Call on each trader individually and make a short presentation for your intended service.

6 Call on a small random sample of the residential areas to sniff out potential interest in your idea.

7 If there is a product or produce involved, do all of the foregoing but also spread some samples around and endeavour to gauge the reaction. This isn't rocket science but what you have to do to establish demand at a low cost.

Doing some research to iron out the wrinkles

Even if the results of your test-marketing fill you with confidence, it is good practice to undertake some additional research to check whether there are still a few wrinkles that need to be ironed out before leaping headlong into tho mnr ketplace. There are several ways you might do this, but here is one that worked for me, and it cost me nothing. I visited the best search engine of them all, www.google.com, to find out everything I could about the feasibility of my idea.

I did this before I launched my part-time self-publishing venture (on which more at the end of this chapter) and located six superb articles, which saved me needless anguish later on. In one of these, I discovered that I could do most of the work on my domestic computer, thus occasioning only minimal outsourcing. This particular article also knocked back some other ham-fisted notions I had been harbouring about getting the business up and running. All of this I could equally have gleaned by conversing with a start-up consultant, but doing it that way would have set me back several hundred pounds.

Getting to the heart of running your own business

Your route map is starting to take shape, and this is where the hard work begins. You should now be thinking in terms of getting to the heart of running your own business by engaging in further research and development before you arrange follow-up meetings with the bank and the small business advisory initiative, after which you ought to be making provision for appointing an accountant and solicitor (if required). The closer you get to what will make your enterprise tick, the more readily you will be able to access assistance from the professionals. There is much still to be done, but lots of assistance is available to help you get there. At the end of this section, I will direct you to an online source offering free tuition on most of the essential aspects of running a business, as well as to a public-sector offline source that may cost you a little but is worth the investment. Let us start, though, with a suggestion for the template of your all-important business plan.

Creating your business plan

Not everyone likes writing reports, and that basically is what your business plan will be: a report. It will be the instrument that not only keeps you focused on your goals, but also attracts any external investment you may require. Borrow a book on the subject from your local public library and learn from an expert. In the meantime, here are some of the basic elements you will want to include.

o Explain exactly how your business idea works in practice.
o Describe your objectives.
o Define the marketplace.
o Research the competition.

- o Produce a clear account of your product or service.
- o Explain the key aspects of your sales policy.
- o Develop a strategy to market the business.
- o Crystallise the strengths and weaknesses of your idea.
- o Make out a case for financial assistance.
- o Show how you will fund the business.
- o Describe the market, its characteristics, and the current trends.
- o Show precisely where your product or service fits in.
- o Summarise the overall content and position it accordingly.

Deciding your business status

You have a choice of routes, and the eventual decision will largely depend on the nature of your retirement business.

Becoming a sole trader

If you are planning to work on your own, your best bet is to become a sole trader. It is the simplest way to own a business and will keep your legal costs to a minimum. You will need to tell the Inland Revenue of your enterprise (unless no revenue is involved). As a sole trader, all the profits from the business will be yours. On the downside, any debt you take on board will also be your responsibility.

Forming a partnership

If you intend to invite other people to become involved as principals, you might want to consider setting up in partnership. This is similar to operating as a sole trader, except that all of the costs and profits are shared between the partners. A partnership can also allow the responsibility and work to be equally shared, which can lessen the pressure on you.

Whatever you decide, draw up a partnership agreement to protect your own interests, bearing in mind that all debt incurred is an individual and collective accountability. Partnership agreements should always include provision for:

o partnership shares;
o partnership property;
o capital;
o drawings;
o accounts;
o restrictions to protect other partners; and
o comprehensive termination provisions to protect ongoing partners.

Forming a limited company

A limited company is a more complicated form of business ownership. As a director of a limited company, you won't be personally responsible for the debts of your business, as a company is separate from its owners. You will pay yourself a salary just like any other employee. However, running a limited company entails very specific rules and regulations, and will require the assistance of a solicitor and accountant. Initial set-up costs will be higher than for a partnership or sole trader, as you will need to register with Companies House and submit regular financial statements.

Choosing a trading name

Choosing a trading name is a crucial exercise that you will need to address as soon as possible. It can make or break any business. List as many ideas as you can before deciding on the name your enterprise is to trade under. Getting it right from the start is essential – you don't want to have to change it after a few months. The secret is to adopt the KISS approach (keep it simple Simon/Sarah).

There are a few house rules to become familiar with before proceeding further. In essence, the ideal trading name should meet these requirements.

1 The core word of the trading name should have no more than seven letters. Preferably, it should have five letters.
2 The core word should have no more than three syllables. Preferably, it should have two syllables.
3 The name should look *and* sound right.
4 It should fit the purpose of the enterprise.
5 It should be legally acceptable.

Using your own name is quite all right and makes sense if you are setting up as a consultant of one type or another. But keep it simple. Don't say 'Humphrey D. Lestocque Insurance Services', but rather 'Lestocque Insurance'. That is, use the core words to best effect. (Note: the first and second requirements mentioned above do not apply to trading names based on your own name.)

There is a lot in a name: get it right from the outset.

Financing your business

You should give prior attention to how much money you need to get started. In fact, you will have to consider very carefully whether you want to enter into any business that entails a considerable financial outlay, at a time in your life when it might be unwise to embrace that sort of commitment. This could discolour your entire business plan; if it will cause you to worry, don't do it. Conversely, if you are converting a lifetime hobby into a business, your investment will probably be very small.

Possible sources of finance include:

1 personal savings;
2 insurance policies;
3 annuities;
4 spare equity in your home;
5 friends and relations;
6 a bank loan; and
7 public-sector assistance.

It is highly unlikely that your bank manager will demonstrate much enthusiasm about handing over hard cash on the strength of a business proposal from a retiree without evidence that there is other funding in place.

Your first port of call should be to the local offices of New Deal 50 plus. Listen to what they have to say, and, if they offer you assistance in any shape or form, take it. Next, pay a visit to your local council's business development unit, where (assuming that your plan is sound and the proposition viable) you may gain access to grants or soft loans that aren't normally broadcast at large. Now you can go to your bank manager ...

Deciding your location

Where you locate will depend on the nature of your retirement business. You must give consideration to premises as you put together your business plan and initial budget. You will need a shop if you are to be a retailer, or a nest factory if you are to be manufacturing something or other in small way. For both of these eventualities go first to the public sector, where you might be offered what you need at a peppercorn rent. Try, though, to locate at home. For most third-age enterprises, a home base is a distinct possibility; it conserves cash and is quite acceptable to most funding sources. If you need a separate phone line or a 'head' office, make appropriate provision in your budgeting.

Staffing your business

Will you be going it alone or will you need staff? Only you and your business idea will determine that. If you need assistance, go first once again to the public sector. They will identify trained personnel (or cover training costs) and provide employment grants where appropriate.

Managing your accounts and cash flow

Do you have basic bookkeeping or accounting skills? If not, consider taking an evening class. Even if you are going to use an accountant, you still need to know the rudiments so as to be able to exercise financial control over your business and manage the cash flow efficiently. An online alternative you might want to consider is Dave Marshall's website (www.coursepal.com/apps/go.php4?id=z81). Dave is a management accountant by profession and offers comprehensive free training for beginners. You can either participate in his tutorial online or download the e-book version to study offline at your own convenience.

Allowing for taxation

Taxation isn't a subject we need to delve into so early in your potential adventure, but it would be prudent to make some allowance for its ensuing inevitability. You should be thinking in terms of:

1 income tax;
2 National Insurance contributions; and
3 VAT (in the fullness of time).

Preparing your accounts

Should your business turnover (total sales) before expenses fall below £15,000 for a full year of trading, you won't be required to provide detailed accounts. Instead, a simple three-line summary will suffice. For example:

Turnover	*£14,657*
Less purchases and expenses	*£5,500*
Net profits	*£9,157*

Marketing your business

There is no mystique about marketing. It is all down to common sense and practical application. Ignore the hype and concentrate on the essentials:

1 costing
2 price-setting
3 buying
4 merchandising
5 selling.

You might also need to think about:

o advertising
o public relations
o exhibitions.

You will find ample practical training online or offline. (See the subsection 'Acquiring general business skills' below.)

Engaging in e-commerce

Unless you intend to take the cyberspace route for marketing your business, put e-commerce (selling on the internet) on the back burner for now. When you do get around to it, don't rely on it as your primary medium for sales. Use it initially for the purpose for which it was invented: as a channel of information, both receivable and deliverable. Doing it this way provides you with two valuable operational devices: the facility to receive information opens the door to ongoing market research, while the facility to deliver information electronically presents you with a cyberspace marketing application.

Using the internet search facilities, you can keep tabs on your competition, source valuable applications and software for free, and keep a constant lookout for new ideas. Using the Net as a marketing application, you can create a powerful website to:

o promote your product or service;
o foster loyalty;
o answer prospects' questions;
o provide them with additional information;
o attract customers; and
o capture email addresses to build a list of potential customers.

You can do all of this and, if you go about matters in the right way, you can achieve your objectives on a limited budget. I recommend that you use the free facility at www.freeservers.com to create your first commercial website. You won't need hypertext mark-up language (HTML) skills, because it is all point-and-click – as easy as ABC.

Taking the cyberspace route

More and more retirees are turning to the internet as a vehicle for operating a small business from home – and with good reason. Start-up costs are minimal (free if you choose to become an affiliate of a global concern) and the bulk of the chores are handled automatically, thus freeing up time to develop the enterprise.

While operating a home-based internet business is a solitary occupation, you will be in good company, because there are millions of you out there in cyberspace. Very soon it won't seem so lonely. You will strike up friendships with all sorts of people you are unlikely ever to meet in person, and you will experience generosity on an unbounded scale. You will be the receiver of freely given advice and practical assistance concerning suitable businesses, affiliate programmes, websites, virtual office suites, domain-name services, e-zines, mailing lists, email facilities, bulk mailers, auto-responders, advertisement tools, and the like – for much of which software you won't be asked to pay.

This is the wonder of operating as an international networker. Show willing and you will get lots of help and encouragement in your quest for success. For detailed information on taking the cyberspace route, refer to my book *Starting an Internet Business at Home* (Kogan Page, 2001).

Acquiring general business skills

If you are short on general business skills, you will need to get up to speed as quickly as possible to make the most of your enterprise. Below you will find valuable online and offline avenues of training. Choose one and apply yourself before you launch your business – even if you are just doing it for pleasure.

Learning online

Go to www.myownbusiness.org, an ultra-professional non-profit website, where you can access completely free of charge a high-calibre online training course on how to go about setting up a business in retirement (Fig 7.1).

The course comes complete with 12 wide-ranging lessons and 33 powerful sound bites (in a variety of digital formats) from successful entrepreneurs, with interactive feedback for each session. You get all of this without having to invest a penny. It covers in depth all of the elements we have just touched on. Even if you aren't on the internet at home, you can still access this comprehensive course for free at your local library. As it doesn't require online participation, you may download or print out the entire programme to study at home in your own time.

Learning offline

Online learning is extremely useful for getting up to speed on theory, but if you are really serious about pursuing a retirement business on a hands-on basis, I would suggest that you put yourself down for one of the many business start-up programmes sponsored by the Department for Work and Pensions. Don't be put off by the maximum age cut-off point. If you are sufficiently persuasive, you will gain admittance.

FREE E-LEARNING FOR ENTREPRENEURS

MY OWN BUSINESS™   Para Español

Our Sponsors | Membership | Tell a friend | Bookmark This Page | Forums & Chat | Newsletter | Hall of Wisdom
Home | About Us | Contact Us | Success Stories | Submit Your Story | On-Line Course | Resources

Tuesday, November 18, 2003   Quote of the day - *Whose Life Is It Anyway? (Brian Clark)*

MY OWN BUSINESS: A FREE INTERNET COURSE ON STARTING A BUSINESS.

Welcome to the world's leading and largest free multilingual Internet course for entrepreneurs!
This website is presented in English and Spanish as a service to anyone starting or operating a business.

Our Mission: We educate entrepreneurs by providing vital information to help them succeed. We believe that success in business leads to prosperity and that prosperity is the solution to many of the problems facing our nation and world.

Your access to financial independence . . .

Too often people fail in business because they make avoidable mistakes! This online, 12-session business course provides the basic do's and don'ts for entrepreneurs.

Fig. 7.1 An interactive business course to get you up to speed on theory

I did, and I did so because, no matter how much you think you know about commerce, you can never learn enough.

Here is an example of a typical syllabus:

o new business planning;
o markets and market selection;
o product identification;
o marketing;
o computer training;
o support systems for start-ups;
o financial planning;
o public-sector funding;
o private-sector funding;
o sourcing proven ideas; and
o legal aspects.

It may cost you a little to participate, but it will be money well spent if your heart is set on starting a business in retirement, whether for fun or profit.

Crucial questions to ask your professional advisers

Armed with all of this intelligence, you will be more than able to field questions from your professional advisers – but here are some crucial ones you might want to ask them.

Your solicitor

1 What are my legal obligations if I opt for sole-trader status?
2 Explain to me the significance of individual and collective responsibility for debts incurred in a partnorohip arrangement.
3 How much will it cost me to set up a limited company?
4 Will I need more than one director?
5 Must I produce an annual return even though my turnover is small?

Your accountant

1 Which accounting books should I keep?
2 Are there different accounting procedures according to business status (sole trader, partnership, and limited company)?
3 What records should I maintain for taxation purposes?
4 How much do I have to be turning over before I register for VAT?
5 How much will you charge me for the annual audit?

Your bank manager

1 Can you provide me with an overdraft facility?
2 If not, what are your best terms for a small business loan?
3 What are your charges for administering a small business current account?
4 If I get lucky and want to place money on deposit, what is the best rate of interest you can offer me?
5 How often do you need to see management accounts (monthly, quarterly, or half-yearly)?

Your public-sector funding contact

1 Do I qualify for a small business grant?
2 Can you offer me a soft loan facility?
3 Tell me about employment grants and how they operate.
4 What are your rental terms for office and factory accommodation?
5 Can I obtain a training grant?
6 What else can you offer me?

Case study

Barbara (68) is named Small Business Person of the Year

Here is inspiration for you. This remarkable woman proved that it is never too late to start your own business. A grandmother of four past retirement age, Barbara Miller transformed a start-up distribution company into a multimillion-dollar venture, despite personal difficulties and setbacks. For Barbara, the going got about as tough as it gets – losing a job, starting a business, and winning a bout with cancer. Her greatest start-up challenge was neither raising capital nor finding a strong management team; rather, it was her health.

With her former colleagues joining in to help out, Barbara pulled her resources together to start her own company. Miller Paper opened its doors with 15 employees. The company, based in Amarillo, Texas, is now a leading wholesale distributor of paper and related products in the Midwest.

Her advice to would-be retiree entrepreneurs: 'Find a niche that puts your customer first, and take care of their needs. Treating people just exactly as you would like to be treated is paramount. Make your customers feel very important – because they are!'

In 2002, Barbara Miller was named Small Business Person of the Year for the state of Texas. None of us will emulate her achievements, but she is an inspiration to anyone thinking about starting a business in retirement.

Personal case study

Most of my retirement businesses are small online ventures, and I operate them for fun. There is an exception though. Thrifty Books is an offline enterprise that I use to self-publish some of my fiction output. Market traders constitute the sole distribution channel and, while I don't make profits, I cover my costs. I also achieve the core objective: my books get read by other people ...

8

Participating in voluntary work

Volunteering your services to benefit the community is a noble gesture to make in retirement. You can do voluntary work at any age. Even if you give just an hour or two a week, you can make a real difference. Whether you want to assist in cleaning up the environment or to help children learn to read, you may find that there is a local opportunity just right for you. You have a range of skills and experience that you have built up over your lifetime, at work and in the course of other activities.

Your skills and experience may prove invaluable to many people and organisations in your community. From helping people who find it difficult to get about with their shopping to providing legal advice for a local charity, you can make a vital contribution to all aspects of community life. With time on your hands in retirement, your skills and experience could be the key to unlocking opportunity for other people less fortunate than yourself, and provide you with a real sense of purpose and achievement. At the same time, volunteering can be good for *you*, enabling you to keep active, meet people, and have fun.

Points to consider before deciding to be a volunteer

Volunteering your services isn't something you should rush into impetuously without due consideration for its implications. Before making contact with *any* voluntary organisation, think about what you want to know from them and what they are likely to ask you.

o How much time can you give?
o At what time of day?
o Will you be fully committed?
o What do you want to gain from volunteering: the satisfaction of helping people, the pleasure of meeting people, or the opportunity to acquire new expertise?
o What existing skills or experience can you offer?
o Will you get out-of-pocket expenses recompensed?
o Does the organisation insure its volunteers?
o Are you receiving any form of state benefit? (You will need to check that your volunteering won't put this at risk.)

Will I be interviewed?

Most voluntary associations will probably not formally interview you before they offer a placement, but they will want to have a relaxed chat. However, if the role has some definitive responsibility (for example, handling money), or if you will be working with people or with dangerous equipment, the interview may be more formal. In either case, this gives you and the voluntary group a chance to assess each other and an opportunity to ask questions. The sort of questions you will be asked will vary from one organisation to another and will depend on the type of voluntary work you are interested in. A typical interviewer, formal or informal, may enquire about any of the following:

o why you are interested in volunteering;
o what sort of voluntary work you are interested in;
o what your particular skills are;
o what new skills you would like to learn through volunteering; and
o how much time you have to offer.

You can ask them anything that you feel unsure about. You may want to check out some or all of these points.

o Are there any opportunities for training or gaining qualifications?
o What variety is there in the work?
o What form of support or supervision can I expect?
o Does volunteering affect any benefits I am claiming?

An informal chat or interview can also give you an opportunity to look at where you will be volunteering and meet some of the other staff and volunteers.

Looking for voluntary work in your local area

There is a standard range of voluntary activities available locally, for example:

o gardening;

o being part of a team planning a fête;

o campaigning; and

o teaching someone to read.

Unless you are already sure what you want to do, it is worth finding out what kind of work there is near where you live. If you are unsure, you can contact relevant concerns directly. For example, if you want to teach, you could contact local schools, colleges, or continuing education centres. Some groups are looking for people with specific skills; others (including volunteer bureaux) will find voluntary work for everyone, including people with extra support needs. Most of the openings for older helpers are based locally, and the best places to look for opportunities are your local volunteer bureau, public library, or daily newspaper. Alternatively, you may create your own opportunities for voluntary work, like the retired villagers in 'Case study 1'.

Case study 1

Village Pride takes on the local litter louts

In the village where I live, a group of retirees became so incensed with the yob culture propensity for dumping litter (and the local council's apparent inability to staunch the problem) that they took matters into their own hands. They formed themselves into a voluntary clean-up service, aptly named Village Pride. At the outset their efforts were regarded with scathing criticism, but gradually the message is beginning to sink in with even the most insensitive among the trash tearaways. Recently, Village Pride was awarded a sizeable annual public-sector grant to boost its meagre funds.

Looking for voluntary work nationwide

The website www.do-it.org.uk contains the national volunteering database, which you can browse for work opportunities in the voluntary sector (Fig. 8.1).

Select a category from the list (featured below) to see what it is all about. The database includes case studies to give you a feel for what might be involved. To make things even easier, each page has a special quick-search tool that will find opportunities just in that category.

o animals
o art and culture
o catering
o children
o disabilities
o disaster relief

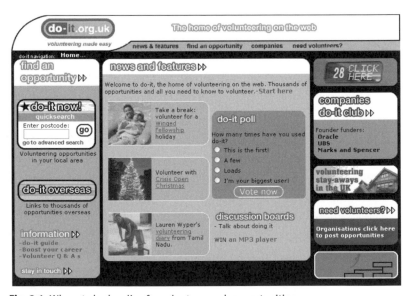

Fig. 8.1 Where to look online for voluntary work opportunities

- o domestic violence
- o drugs and addictions
- o elderly
- o employment
- o entertainment
- o environment
- o health, hospitals, and hospices
- o heritage
- o human and civil rights
- o legal aid and justice
- o mentoring
- o museums
- o music
- o politics.

Suggestions for voluntary work

Join the Retired and Senior Volunteer Programme

The Retired and Senior Volunteer Programme (RSVP) numbers around 8,000 volunteers nationwide, who take part in a wide range of activities. Voluntary work involving the environment has become more popular and participants help disabled people with their gardening, teach horticultural skills to young people, create wild flower sites, clear walkers' pathways, and much more besides. A group of older volunteers, some of whom live in a care home, produce knitwear for children in need at home and abroad.

The RSVP initiative is run by the Community Service Volunteers (CSV), with the aim of providing opportunities for people over 50 across the UK to become involved in their communities as volunteers. Typical RSVP activities include:

o helping with reading in schools;

o helping in hospitals and health centres;

o transporting patients;

o collecting prescriptions;

o setting up and running lunch clubs;

o befriending housebound people; and

o carrying out environmental work.

RSVP is for all retirees who want to volunteer, whatever their interests, state of health, or area of residence. You don't need any experience or qualifications, just a desire to help other people.

Phone 020 643 1385 or visit www.csv-rsvp.org.uk to find out more about RSVP's operations in England and Wales. Phone 0131 622 7766 or visit www.csv-rsvpscotland.org.uk to find out more about RSVP's operations in Scotland.

Reach out to others less fortunate

REACH supports the development of thousands of voluntary concerns by recruiting older volunteers from all backgrounds and finding them the right voluntary-sector placement to match their skills and expertise. If you have skills to offer, you can help. Phone 020 7582 6543 or visit www.reach-online.org.uk for more details.

Case study 2

Emmanuel benefits from volunteering his commercial skills

Emmanuel Nnatuanya is one of many people who registered with REACH during 2001. Highly qualified in the financial world, he has held several responsible posts in Nigeria and the UK. Already involved in voluntary work, Emmanuel was looking for another outlet for his skills and experience, and heard about REACH from the National Council for Voluntary Organisations and the National Coalition for Black Volunteering.

'I am now working as a voluntary consultant and business adviser to a nursery school in Hackney,' says Emmanuel. 'I thought they should expand, so I decided to help them prepare a business plan, so that they could open a new nursery school.'

Enlist with the Experience Corps

The Experience Corps aims to encourage a quarter of a million people aged 50 and over to volunteer to help develop their local communities. There are thousands of opportunities available, and the Experience Corps is especially interested in people coming forward with their own ideas for projects. Retirees are especially invited to become involved. Phone 0800 10 60 80 or visit www.experiencecorps.co.uk for more information.

Case study 3
John finds volunteering uplifting
Artist John Wiggins contacted the Experience Corps after ending up with time on his hands following retirement.

'I've been running art classes for local people, some of whom suffer from mental-health illnesses. I found painting helped distract people from their problems – it works therapeutically. At times, you saw people improving, and I found that I got a real uplift from my efforts.'

Lend a helping hand at Rubka

Rubka is a voluntary organisation that focuses on help-ing elderly people to stay independent. Many of our elderly citizens are forced to cope alone with financial and personal worries. Often they have nobody to turn to for company and support. This is when the friendship of a voluntary visitor can make all the difference. Volunteers help by:

1 keeping in contact with the people that Rukba helps and visiting them at least twice a year;
2 providing a friendly voice on the phone;
3 raising awareness locally about the help that Rukba offers; and
4 joining in fund-raising activities.

Just a few hours a month is all you need to volunteer for Rukba, and you will be supported by a local representa-tive. Contact Nicholas Tuck on 020 7605 4224 or email NTuck@rukba.org.uk if you would like to know more.

Case study 4

Karen visits people who love to talk to her

Karen Collins, a Rubka volunteer for Basingstoke, has made firm friends with the people she visits.

She says, 'At first I wondered, "What do you talk to older people about?" Then I discovered that they love to talk to you. There is plenty of laughter and the most important thing is to be there as a friend.'

Help out at the Citizens' Advice Bureau

The largest independent advice-giving network in the world is provided through a network of some 3,000 outlets in England, Scotland, Wales, and Northern Ireland. The Citizens' Advice Bureau provides free, confidential, impartial, and independent advice to everyone regardless of race, gender, disability, or sexual orientation. There are opportunities to volunteer in all Citizens' Advice Bureaux as advisers (accredited training available), trustees, administrators, and social policy workers. Some bureaux also have openings for volunteers in fund-raising, public relations, community liaison, and IT coordination. Visit www.citizensadvice.org.uk to find out more about getting involved or refer to your phone book for the nearest bureau.

Become involved with Age Concern

Age Concern cares about all older people and finds effective ways to make later life more fulfilling and enjoyable for them. Locally, a network of 14,000 groups and 250,000 volunteers provides community-based services such as lunch clubs, day centres, and home-visiting. Nationally, Age Concern campaigns on ageing issues, undertakes research, provides information and advice, and offers a wide range of training. Email ace@org.uk or visit www.ace.org.uk for details of your nearest group.

Make an impact on asthma

Asthma UK is an independent charity dedicated to conquering asthma. It funds asthma research, offers information and advice, and campaigns for a better deal for people with asthma. The charity has launched a programme called 'Make an Impact', which relies on volunteers to promote the charity's services, contribute to campaigning, and encourage others to get involved in the work. Details of the programme are available in an easy-to-read pack, with step-by-step instructions. Volunteers are based at home, working flexible hours (approximately two hours per week) for three to six months. Visit www.asthma.org.uk for more information.

Personal case study

I don't do as much as perhaps I ought in the way of voluntary work, but for several years I was associated with the Kidney Research Fund and nowadays I always endeavour to stretch out a hand where it is needed. For example, I am currently in the process of setting up a voluntary association to assist tenants who are being unfairly treated by their landlords.

If you would like to find rewarding and fulfilling work in charities and voluntary organisations, then I would recommend that you read Craig Brown's *Working in the Voluntary Sector* (How To Books, 2002).

9

Why writing up your experiences can benefit others

Writing is something else you may have considered in the past, but never got around to doing anything constructive about. Perhaps you thought it might prove too difficult; perhaps you even thought that what you had to say would be of little or no interest to anyone else. If so, you would be wrong on both counts. There is plenty of help available with regard to structuring your thoughts as the subject matter for a book, website, or other medium. Irrespective of the nature of your life experiences, there is a market for them. Find this hard to believe? Read on. It could lead to an absorbing project that will enrich your retirement and provide inspiration for others following in your footsteps.

Mastering the mental blocks

There is an age-old adage that is as true today as when it was first mooted: 'Everyone has at least one good book in them.' The problem is that most people never get around to writing it, because they hamper progress by cluttering their minds with blocks. Could you produce a self-help book in your third-age years that would be of benefit to others? With professional guidance you probably could – and there is a plethora of assistance available on the internet for free. Just tap 'creative writing assistance' into the search engine www.google.com and it will come up with tens of thousands of sources. I never suspected I would, but I have managed to produce several such books on a part-time basis in my retirement years, and so could you if you set about matters with conviction.

So you have never written anything creative?

It is not true to say that you have never written anything creative; you know you have. You have been doing so all of your life. When you were sitting exams at school, you were engaging in the creative writing process, addressing questions and providing answers with well-reasoned arguments. When you sit down to compose a letter, produce a thesis, or develop a business proposal, you are in the creative mode. All of these exercises have something in common: they are works of non-fiction, and so it follows that the creation of a full-length book in that genre is any and all of these activities writ large. You are adept at creative writing, but so far you have only skimmed the surface of your latent ability.

Case study 1

Jo discovers she can write non-fiction

I was recently approached by Jo Hedges, a retired lady living in South Africa, for advice on how to approach a writing opportunity she had been presented with out of the blue. Here is an extract from her correspondence with me:

I have been contacted by an editor of a country-style magazine. She wants an article on the area where I live in South Africa. I did not know how to even begin and had offered to submit something on the life/lifestyle in Guinea (absolutely non-existent and third world of the worst kind imaginable). She was not interested, yet with your tutorial I feel motivated to work on the South African article and hope to convince her also on the piece on West Africa. You hit the nail spot on when you say one does write non fiction all the time when one does reports, writes CVs, sends emails to friends and family, and writes letters. Thank you very much for your assistance, Jim.

So you have tried again and again without success?

Perhaps, on the other hand, you have been activating your intrinsic skills for years, and all you have to show for it is a never-ending stream of rejection slips. Perhaps, too, you have been focusing your energies on fiction, the most notoriously difficult of genres to break into as a writer aspiring to achieve the recognition that leads to publication. Could it be that you have now decided the only way you will ever see your work in print is to become a self-publisher?

You wouldn't be the first. These famous masters of fiction were all obliged to take the route of shelling out hard cash to have their debut novels printed:

o Alexandre Dumas
o D.H. Lawrence
o Edgar Allan Poe
o Edgar Rice Burroughs
o George Bernard Shaw
o Gertrude Stein
o James Joyce
o John Grisham
o Mark Twain
o Mary Baker Eddy
o Rudyard Kipling
o Stephen Crane
o Upton Sinclair
o Virginia Woolf
o Walt Whitman
o William Blake
o Zane Grey.

Incidentally, John Grisham sold copies of his first novel, *A Time to Kill*, out of the boot of a car, which at the outset was his sole 'vehicle' for distribution ...

But we are concerned here with another genre, a genre that permits self-expression under predetermined guidelines designed to give you a more than even chance of publication without the necessity of paying for the privilege, providing always that your work and its presentation are painstakingly and professionally executed.

Testing your aptitude for writing non-fiction

Ask yourself these questions and spend a few minutes in quiet reflection before you provide the answers.

1 Do you like to read, be it fiction or non-fiction?
2 Do you enjoy writing letters, reports, or whatever?
3 Do you have an above-average vocabulary?
4 Do you strive at every opportunity to enhance your personal word power?
5 Do you persist with crosswords until you have solved all the clues?
6 Do you have an enquiring mind?
7 Do you have special interests?
8 Do you have expertise in any particular subject(s)?
9 Would you undertake research to confirm what you *think* you know?
10 Would you be prepared to share this knowledge with others?
11 Would you be willing to make time to write about it?
12 Are you comfortable about committing your private thoughts to paper?
13 Are you self-disciplined?
14 Are you relaxed about working on your own?

If you can genuinely answer 'Yes' to all of these questions, you already have a strong aptitude for creating niche non-fiction in the shape of self-help books.

If on the other hand you answered 'Yes' to most and 'No' to a few, then work on those negative areas.

If you answered 'No' to question 8, then think again and dig deeply this time. Most people have expert knowledge on something or other that has emerged from personal experience. It could be a job, a hobby, or any of a thousand disparate topics. *Should you consider that what you know would be of little value to anyone else, you would be wrong.* Many people share a passion for your particular area of interest and are anxious to become even better informed.

Case study 2

Terry (73) passes on his wisdom

An ex-RAF colleague of mine, Terry Barefoot, has had a lifelong love affair with freshwater fishing. For years he contemplated writing up an account of his experiences. Now in retirement he has gone one better by producing a full-length book, in which to pass on his accumulated wisdom to younger enthusiasts on the same wavelength. Terry tells me he has found a publisher for his first work and has three more similar projects lined up.

Cashing in on introspection

Introspection as a discipline for writing self-help literature? Very much so, if you are to be writing all you can in that genre, be it for offline or online consumption. In odd moments, think over what you think you know for sure, and then put it to the test in small ways. For example, your project is embroidery and you are utterly convinced that a certain style of cross-stitching, which is to be a cornerstone of your teaching, is well within the capability of any novice. But is it? And how can you confirm your conviction? Visit the local public library and access several books on the topic (you will find plenty). Compare alternative viewpoints to establish if you are on the right track or if, at this early stage, you should rethink your strategy. Writing self-help literature is niche-carving; to be certain that your exposition of a topic will be convincing, you must be forever in touch with your thoughts and feelings as you construct the basic tenets.

Cultivating innate intuition

Introspection leads us neatly on to another essential discipline: making the most of your intuition. Intuition is an incredible weapon to have at your command as a writer. But intuition doesn't just happen; you can't switch it on at will, until you first learn how to cultivate your innate power by listening to your inner voice. There are several excellent works on the subject – including Sylvia Clare's *Trusting Your Intuition* (How To Books, 1999) – but here are some basic pointers to help you get started on your quest to hear your inner voice.

Slow down

Information is proliferating at such a frenzied rate today that, even with PCs and mobile phones (or perhaps because of them), your attention is stretched to the extreme. Not only do you have more facts about more fields of information than ever before, but you are also subject to a greater array of opinions.

Fortunately, beneath all the cacophony of the information age, the quiet truth about problem-solving and decision-making is always available to you. By learning to slow down and pay attention to what is right under your nose, you have a chance to find your own authentic answers, unaided by media and technology. To do that, you must build up your 'intuition muscle' and learn to centre yourself in the present moment. It is only at your core, in the here-and-now eye of the global information hurricane, that you can hear your inner voice.

Become attuned to the subtle messages all around you

How attuned are you to the subtle messages all around you, like those hidden behind your spoken communication? There is guidance available to you at all times, just below the surface of logic, just after you stop pushing and striving, just before you jump to conclusions. By cultivating the ability to pause and be comfortable with silence, and then by focusing steadily, listening for the first sounds, and feeling for your first impressions, you can help your intuition wake up suddenly and enthusiastically, as if from a long winter's sleep.

In my own searching to cultivate my inner voice, I have learned to listen for the faintest of whispers, the nearly silent song. One of the most important skills in developing accurate intuition is the ability to tone down your domineering talk-addicted mind, which arrogantly thinks it knows how the world works without ever observing what is happening in the freshly occurring present moment. To know clearly, you must learn to observe neutrally, and true observation can only take place with a silent mind.

Soften your awareness

Activating intuition always starts with a downward gear shift into softness and silence. You will never receive accurate information with a chattering mind, clenched as tight as a fist. Recall how you feel when you are concentrating and worrying about finishing a project you have set yourself. Your brow is furrowed, you are shackled to the task in hand, and you are probably way ahead of yourself, anxious to achieve the intended goal. This is your 'masculine mind' in operation: the kind of awareness men and women alike must use to achieve concrete results. You are in your linear, left-brained masculine mind so often, you have come to identify it as normal and you tend to forget that there is an equally powerful, complementary state of consciousness that is quiet, unhurried, highly creative, and tension-free: the 'feminine mind' or right brain. The feminine mind isn't goal-oriented; it simply observes, includes, appreciates, and is present in whatever it notices.

Cultivate your intuition, and it will serve you well in every writing assignment you undertake.

Injecting best-selling potential into your work

Is it possible to inject best-selling potential into a work of non-fiction? It certainly is, and some successful writers of how-to literature consciously use the technique wherever and whenever feasible, while many others include it unwittingly but to equally good effect.

Fathoming the secret of best-selling potential

The secret of best-selling potential for how-to and self-help books is to steer clear of the seasonality factor when choosing a topic from your life experiences. This sounds like a contradiction in terms, but it isn't. A topic can be current but with inherent strands of durability attached; conversely, a topic that is seasonal is almost inevitably a fad or fashion, at best transient in nature.

Put another way, the secret is about the identification of longevity. Uncomplicated as this little secret is, it is never easy to apply in practice and calls for concentrated effort, in which introspection, intuition, and research all have a part to play.

Choosing an appealing and enduring topic

As you set about the task of choosing a topic, be on the lookout for the elusive ingredient that might hallmark your work as more than just another one-off.

1 Does the topic have appeal for both sexes?
2 Is the topic of interest to most age groups?
3 Does the topic cut across the socio-economic spectrum?
4 Is the topic readily recognisable?
5 Is the topic niche-carving?
6 Does the topic possess a timeless quality?
7 Are there other books available on the topic?

On the face of it, you may think this is a rather tall order and a constraint on anyone setting out to produce their first book in retirement, even though satisfying five or six of these requirements is still OK for instilling longevity. But if you wish your work to incorporate best-selling potential, these are the questions you should be asking when choosing a topic for consideration. Even if you have already settled on one and are now doubtful whether it would meet these qualifications, look again at your topic from every angle to uncover *any* trace of potential durability. To assist you, here are a few examples of themes that always seem to meet the test of time:

o bookkeeping
o building self-confidence
o buying a guesthouse
o buying a second home
o changing careers
o constructing a business plan
o coping with stress
o handling interviews
o improving your memory
o living abroad
o making a speech
o making a will

o making money from property
o managing other people
o managing your finances
o managing yourself
o mastering business terminology
o overcoming depression
o passing exams
o preparing reports
o retiring from the workplace
o retiring abroad
o returning to work
o self-assertion
o setting up a business
o surviving redundancy
o using the internet
o working abroad
o writing assignments
o writing CVs
o writing essays.

The list is by no means exhaustive. There are others, many others, and yours may be among them.

Everything here scores highly on the seven-point test (listed above) for uncovering the elusive ingredient of a best-seller – as does the book you are currently reading and my two best-sellers *Starting Your Own Business* (How To Books, 2002) and *Starting an Internet Business at Home* (Kogan Page, 2001). Why? Because the market for each of these tomes is like a bottomless pit; there will always be someone else about to travel the respective route and in need of a road map. So, too, might your topic pass the seven-point test if you dissect it thoroughly enough.

Developing your own slant on a given topic

The ability to develop your own slant on a given topic also contributes to best-selling potential. Everyone has their own way of looking at things and describing how they work. When Napoleon Hill and Clement Stone got together to produce the famous self-help book *Think and Grow Rich* (1937), they took the timeless and much-worked concept of mind over matter and subjected it to the twist of two disparate but complementary viewpoints. Interestingly, although both names appear on the cover, there was only one author, Napoleon Hill, the architect of the slant that transformed their work into a best-selling book, spanning nearly seven decades in worldwide bookshops. If you can find an unusual angle, a different approach, or a hitherto unworked technique for your topic, you are on the way to developing the unique quality that will set your work apart from similar tomes.

Writing as a memento for your grandchildren

If, like me, you don't get to see your grandchildren very often because they live far away, you might want to set down your experiences as a memento for them in a self-published book: who you are, what you are, and *why* you are who you are and what you are. I have got this on my list of things to do with a notional title of *Grandpa's Story.*

Here are two helpful tips, should this approach appeal to you.

1 Back to our trusty online detective www.google.com – type in as a keyword phrase 'writing my life story' and watch what happens. You will be directed to thousands of creditable sources for professional advice on con-

structing and writing up your material. Alternatively, refer to Michael Oke's *Writing Your Life Story* (How To Books, 2001).

2 Purchase a copy of Peter Domanski and Philip Irvine's *A Practical Guide to Publishing Books Using Your PC* (Domanski–Irvine Book Company, 1997). You won't find this invaluable guide at your local bookshop. Instead, send a cheque or postal order for £12.99 to Domanski–Irvine Book Company, Coldwell Farm, Stretfordbury, Leominister, Herefordshire HR6 0QL. Alternatively, email info@dibookco.u-net.com for further details.

Creating a dedicated website

Imparting your wisdom needn't necessarily take the shape of a book. You could create a dedicated website, such as the one currently being developed by Vic Wright that is featured in 'Case study 3'. This is proving a popular route with many retirees, because it is less demanding and permits of one-to-one interfacing with like-minded visitors. Should this be of interest to you (and it is worth investigating) you might consider investing in the all-in-one tool that I use. It will set you back around £300, but what you receive for your money is awesome. 'Site Build It' is available for immediate download on a trial basis at http://buildit.sitesell.com/interactive1.html and is *totally inclusive* of the following beneficial features:

o domain name registration;
o hosting;
o brainstorming tools;
o power keyword research and analysis;
o graphic tools;

o point-and-click page-building;

o a choice of page templates;

o file transfer protocol (FTP);

o a form builder/auto-responder;

o data transfer;

o web-based email;

o a newsletter publishing facility;

o brainstorming and research tools;

o a spam checker;

o daily traffic statistics and analysis;

o search engine optimisation;

o automatic search engine submission;

o automatic search engine tracking;

o automatic search engine ranking;

o pay-per-click research;

o mass bidding on keywords;

o four separate traffic headquarters;

o an action guide and a fast-track guide;

o integrated online help;

o an express e-zine to keep you up to date;

o tips and techniques;

o customer support;

o a facility for uploading and downloading; and

o digitised data.

Alternatively, you could opt for a free page-building and hosting service (but that is all you will get), for which there are several sources. Of these, www.freeservers.com is the best.

Case study 3

Vic advises on how to enjoy the third age

Vic Wright, retired and living in Bath, has set up a website (www.mytimesmyown.com) together with an informative on-line newsletter, aimed at providing retirees with ideas and tips on how to enjoy the third age as fully as possible (Fig. 9.1).

Based on his life experiences, Vic produces most of the material himself. He also publishes high-quality articles from expert sources and accepts contributions from subscribers to the newsletter.

Vic says, 'It's early days yet, but I hope that in time it will prove to be an interesting, informative, and sometimes contentious forum for the growing number of senior citizens on the web. I want to get the message across that retirement is an opportunity for personal development, and a time to do all those things you've always wanted to do.'

My Time's My Own

Welcome to Vic's Retirement Site

FREEDOM AT LAST

YOUR SAY

Retired? Now's the time to enjoy yourself and catch up on all those things you wanted to do but never had time for. Time for a new lifestyle.

ARTICLES

This site and its newsletter aim to give you some ideas and tips on how to enjoy your retirement as fully as possible.

ABOUT ME

WHAT DO YOU NEED TO ENJOY YOUR RETIREMENT?

TIIBITS

A Load of Money?

⊠

Obviously it helps, but it's not absolutely necessary. We all know miserable, well-off retirees. But I suspect you also know some poor ones who are enjoying life to the full.

A Stimulating Activity?

Definitely. Better still, make that *activities*. Invest your time in a number of things that you *enjoy* doing. If for some reason you find that you can't do one thing, you'll always have an alternative to fall back on.

Fig. 9.1 Vic Wright's personal retirement website

Here is the mission statement that appears on Vic's home page:

What do you need to enjoy your retirement?

A load of money? *Obviously it helps but it isn't absolutely necessary. We all know miserable, well-off retirees. But I suspect you also know some poor ones who are enjoying life to the full.*

A stimulating activity? *Definitely, but better still, make it* activities. *Invest your time in a number of things that you enjoy doing. If for some reason you find that you can't do one thing, you will always have an alternative to fall back on.*

Friends? *If they have got a positive outlook on life, have a sense of humour and are fun to be with, you can't have too many. Moaners, whiners and the like tend to drag you down. If you can't reform them, it might be best to avoid them.*

Good health? *Great if you've got it. But there is still plenty of fun stuff to do if you haven't.*

Vic's aims in writing up his experiences are exactly in line with those of *Your Retirement Masterplan*: actualising lifetime goals in retirement by enacting a plan for fulfilment in the third age.

Personal case study

Like the works of Terry Barefoot and Vic Wright, my books and websites have a single purpose in mind: imparting what little I know for the benefit of others. Think about what you know, what pearls of wisdom you have accumulated over the years, and then set about establishing your own route for passing on knowledge. When you do that with sincerity, you will experience a unique and humbling sense of fulfilment. Can you really become successful writing up your experiences as a part-time activity in retirement? In all modesty, I am living proof that you can; I have far too many other interests to make a full-time career out of writing. Even so, I wouldn't have persisted with writing on a part-time basis unless it was affording me fulfilment. You will recall reading this statement when the first flush of recognition comes your way. It is addictive!

Let me show you what I mean by way of an example. I took a break from writing this section and typed into www.google.com the keywords 'starting an internet business'. On the first page, up came one of my books, *Starting an Internet Business at Home*, ranking at no. 1 out of 5.6 million entries. I then proceeded to www.amazon.com and inserted the same keywords into their search engine for books. Up again came the same title, ranking at no. 3 out of 27,376 competing titles. The searches also work with names when your writing achieves recognition. I typed my own name into www.google.com and up came 3.5 million entries under 'Jim Green'. Ranking at no. 13 was *Starting Your Own Business* and a little further on at no. 38 was *Starting an Internet Business at Home*.

Think about it, and then make a start on writing up your own experiences. It could prove one of the most rewarding experiences of your retirement years. It works for me (and I'm no Norman Vincent Peale); it could just as easily work for you.

10

Taking the hobby route to self-actualisation

It is good practice to have at least one hobby in retirement but better to have two, because then (as Vic Wright confirms) when your interest in one temporarily wanes, you can always switch to the other for refreshment. Some retirees would appear to focus most of their energies in this direction and, in so doing, take the hobby route to self-actualisation. No bad thing. A passion for leisure pursuits can often replace the void experienced on departing the full-time workplace.

Read the 'Review of more than 50 popular retirement hobbies' below, to ascertain whether anything takes your fancy. Always remember: only you can devise the masterplan for enactment. If hobbies take centre stage, so be it. This is your retirement and your life.

How to match a hobby to your needs

Here are some questions you might want to ask yourself before you select a retirement hobby.

1 Will I really enjoy this hobby?
2 Can I afford it?
3 Am I physically able to become involved?
4 Do I have enough room at home to accommodate the hobby?
5 Does the hobby allow me to retain my privacy?
6 Does the hobby provide opportunities to work with others?
7 Do I really have time for the hobby?
8 Can I develop the necessary skill to do the hobby?

Assessing the enjoyment factor

To settle for a retirement hobby that does no more than fill in time is less than satisfactory. It must provide you with some benefit, some enrichment, some joy that will add colour to your third-age adventure. Use enjoyment as the benchmark when evaluating potential hobbies.

Assessing the cost factor

Preferably, the hobby should cost little or nothing. Few of us third-age people can afford to splash out on leisure pursuits, but fortunately there is no requirement for indulgence. Only a handful of the popular retirement hobbies reviewed below will cost you more than pin money.

Assessing the health factor

Your state of health is also a consideration but it needn't prove a barrier, because there are lots of hobby options for those who are unable to get about as well as they used to. The options include reading, sewing, writing, and website creation.

Assessing the space factor

Unless you are hell-bent on pursuing some project that requires above-average floor space, avoid options that take up too much room. Select your hobby to match your own requirements, but always ensure you have enough space to accommodate it. You don't want to turn your home into a retirement warehouse ...

Assessing the privacy factor

Many retirees enjoy their own company, so if you fall into this category, choose a hobby where you exercise total control. Hands-on creative writing is a good example.

Assessing the company factor

For some retirees the opportunity to work with others is paramount. Choose the more social options from the hobbies reviewed below.

Assessing the time factor

Make time; your time is your own now. Life is too short to miss out on anything that will add enjoyable new dimensions to the third plateau of the lifespan.

Assessing the skill factor

You have a lifetime of accumulated experience to draw upon in developing any necessary skill. Browse through the hobbies below and see if you can find one that is just right for you.

Review of more than 50 popular retirement hobbies

o **Antique restoration:** This hobby requires considerable patience – a quality you may need to develop. For those who love beautiful woods and like to see them at their lustrous best, each refinished piece is a triumph.

o **Aquariums:** A good all-round website for anyone thinking of expanding their aquarium, or just starting out, is Fishkeeping UK (www.fishkeepinguk.co.uk). It provides an extensive directory of national associations, importers, retailers, and web-based clubs.

o **Art:** Everyone has to start somewhere. If you are a beginner, Teaching Art (www.teachingart.co.uk), a leading producer of art training videos, has chosen a range of videos to help those new to painting or who are trying a fresh medium or subject. There are over 100 videos to choose from, including *Oils for Beginners, Watercolour Landscapes in England, Seascapes in California, Chinese Brush,* and *Gardens in Pastel.*

o **Artificial flowers:** They are made from special papers, ribbons, fabrics, buttons, beads, and even shells. You could earn some pin money from this hobby, because of the growing demand from local retailers who use the produce to add ambience to their outlets.

o **Astronomy:** A great website for the budding astronomer is UK250 (www.uk250.co.uk). It lists all the astronomy websites you could possibly need. Find out about the world of astronomy and learn what you need to become an amateur stargazer. If you are interested, Cosmicdust (www.cosmicdust.com) offers a diary of celestial events so that you can plan your gazing with ease – without equipment even. However, if you do want to get the full kit, try Beacon Hill Telescopes (www.beaconhilltelescopes.mcmail.com), one of the UK's leading suppliers, who offer a large selection and low prices.

o **Basketry:** An ancient craft dating back to the dawn of time. Basket-makers often combine their hobbies with nature lore, and spend hours gathering and preparing natural materials for their projects.

o **Beadwork:** Beads date back to the earliest of times. They are made of seeds, shells, glass, metal, wood, plastic, and precious and semi-precious stones. This hobby requires good eyesight, but is typically clean and inexpensive.

o **Bookbinding:** Simple sewing skills, exactness, and love for books are all this hobby requires.

o **Bridge:** The best word to describe the English Bridge Union website (www.ebu.co.uk) is exhaustive. This is definitely the website for an experienced player thinking of entering tournaments, who wants to know the exact rules of bridge. A rather easier website for someone wishing to pick up the game as a hobby is Card Games (www.pagat.com), which tells you the rules of play for rubber, duplicate, and Chicago bridge. You can also visit the Card Games home page for information on other card games.

o **Calligraphy:** Easier than drawing or painting, calligraphy (or 'beautiful writing') is making a comeback, especially among retirees. No one is too old to take up and enjoy this simple hobby, which trains both eye and wrist, and can be pursued equally well from your armchair or bed. You can use calligraphy simply to improve your handwriting, and make it beautiful and legible, or you can letter greetings cards, wedding invitations, and so on.

o **Camping:** Camping can run the gamut from the extremely primitive to the luxurious; you should pick the type that best suits your temperament, camping skills, and wallet. Camping sites are easily accessible from most places, and you can pick up a directory at most bookshops.

o **Candle-making:** Candle-making is enjoying a burgeoning popularity as a craft and as a retiree hobby. Only a few simple materials and tools are required to make your own handsome candles.

o **Caning:** Caning, the making of furniture with cane, is almost a lost art. Anyone looking for an interesting hobby with some income possibilities would do well to investigate caning.

o **Clowning:** If you have ever had a secret yearning to be on stage, now is your chance. As a clown, you can escape into a world of fantasy and give untold pleasure to children and grown-ups in homes and hospitals.

o **Collecting:** Collector Online (www.collectoronline.com) provides the most complete listing on collectors' clubs. Using the search facility is easy – just click on the letter you want to search and check the listings for clubs. It was on this website that I discovered a football medal I acquired in my youth is now a collectable worth several hundred pounds. Collect only what you love, what you have room for, and what you can afford. For example:

o stamps

o coins

o rocks and minerals

- o books
- o prints
- o medals
- o butterflies
- o shells.

o **Cooking:** The culinary arts are growing in popularity, especially among men (myself included). If cooking appeals to you, why not try a few of the basic recipes favoured by your family and close friends, and invite them to serve as guinea pigs for your gourmet treats?

o **Crosswords:** You can find plenty of crosswords of all standards on the web, and many other puzzles too. A good starting point is http://home.freeuk.net/dharrison/puzzles/ which provides puzzles and forums. If you are looking for help in solving a puzzle, try One Across (www.oneacross.com), which provides suggestions. If you want to develop your own crosswords, you might like to review special software available at Crossword Compiler (www.crosswordcompiler.com). Also, take a look at Questique (www.questique.co.uk), a strategy crossword game for up to four players. A simple handicapping system allows children and adults to compete as equals.

o **Digital photography:** Scanners are currently available for less than £100, and digital cameras delivering almost photographic quality can now also be purchased at affordable prices. Digital photography provides some unique benefits: an instant review of your pictures, the ability to edit them on your PC, and the opportunity to publish them on the web or email them to friends and relations (refer back to 'Case study 8' in Chapter 4 for an illustration of how one retiree excels in this hobby). To learn more about all aspects of digital photography, visit ShortCourses (www.shortcourses.com), which provides concise explanations of products and techniques. Armed with this information, you can check out the latest cameras at Image Acquire (www.image-acquire.com).

o **Dramatics:** This hobby involves more than just acting. Each play needs its readers, directors, set designers, stagehands, carpenters, prompters, and publicity staff. Lack of acting talent or skill is no excuse for not participating in dramatics.

o **Drawing, painting, and sculpture:** Look into these arts, even if you think you have no talent. Sign up for lessons. You may be surprised at the results. At the very least, you will find that an increased sensitivity to shape and composition will make you view the world through new eyes; at the most, you will find a rewarding pursuit to enrich your retirement.

o **Fishing:** Where to Fish (www.where-to-fish.com), as its name suggests, is a website devoted to finding the best fishing spots worldwide, for all different kinds of fishing.

o **Gardening:** A great idea if you have time on your hands is to invest some of it in making your garden something to be very proud of. TheGarden (www.thegarden.co.uk) boasts an impressive list of services: hints and tips in the 'Shed', a retail and wholesale directory in the 'Nursery', and information on gardening services and products in 'Services'. The 'Shed' page contains not only tips, but also links to other gardening websites and a directory of gardens you can visit. Gardening UK (www.letsgogardening.co.uk) really is a one-stop gardening website for all your needs. It has the latest gardening articles, weather reports, questions and answers, tips, details of shops and products, news about clubs and shows, and stories about gardening personalities. There is enough reading here for a whole wet summer!

o **Gem-cutting:** You don't need to be a geology graduate to enjoy this hobby. Appreciation for beauty of colour and design, and the patience to work with a specimen until its full potential of beauty is realised, are what it takes. Not all lapidaries hunt out their own specimens, so you don't have to be a rock hound to enjoy gem-cutting.

o **Genealogy:** Genealogy, the study of your family history, is one of the most popular uses of the web. There are a lot of websites to choose from, but here are some that are particularly good. One Name (www.one-name.org) specialises in tracing the history of a particular surname, and has links to groups that can help you make searches. AOL Hometown (www.hometown.aol.com) gives lists and contact addresses for research websites and record offices across the UK. It also links to maps and gazetteers, as well as to websites that publish historical research and explain older dating and calendar systems. UK Genealogy (www.ukgenealogy.co.uk) is the portal for UK genealogical research. Family Search (www.familysearch.org/) hosts a worldwide database of births, deaths, and marriages. Searches of the database are free and will return lists of names that match your criteria, plus links to other relatives. Obviously the database doesn't contain records for everyone who has ever lived, but it is worth a search. (Note: records are only available for those who died more than 100 years ago.)

o **Graphology:** Can analysis of someone's handwriting really indicate their personality? Graphology has become increasingly popular as a partial selection method for jobs, but it is also an interesting retirement hobby and relatively easy to learn. Have a look at Handwriting Analysis (www.handwriting.org). The purpose of this web page is to promote awareness, understanding, and support for handwriting analysis, and to provide a central source of information. Links are supplied to related websites that may be of interest. The British Institute of Graphology home page (www.britishgraphology.org) contains information about tuition, as well as helpful links.

o **History:** If you are interested in history, then it is well worth taking a look at www.bbc.co.uk/history.

o **Home-brewing:** If you have ever fancied being an amateur brewer, then Tom and Vince's Homebrew Site (www.alpha-byte.demon.co.uk) is a great, friendly website to start out from. The website is designed to help you learn the basics of home-brewing, as well as advanced skills and how to produce top-quality home brew. There are links to many other websites that cover different aspects, but all you need to know should be right here with Tom and Vince. They have lists of suppliers of the kind of equipment you will need, as well as details of books that cover this topic.

o **Jewellery-making:** This hobby can be confined to a relatively small space and requires no great outlay of money for tools and materials. It is wise, however, to work with a teacher at the beginning, since there are tricks to soldering, setting stones, and working with metal. Jewellery-making is also a potentially good income producer for the enthusiastic retiree.

o **Juggling:** Why not learn juggling? Not only can you amuse and astound your friends, but you can also improve your coordination and balance. Juggling (www.juggling.org) is the main website for jugglers on the internet. It has listings for clubs, societies, events, magazines, and software. Most importantly, it has lessons on how to juggle clubs, balls, hoops, and anything else you can think of. The lessons have illustrations and are easy to follow, and there are online catalogues for you to order from. Jugglenow (www.jugglenow.com) is another fun website.

o **Kites:** Kiteworld (www.kiteworld.co.uk) is the home of kite-flying on the Net. It has everything for the kite enthusiast, but if you aren't too serious about the topic, then try Clem's Kites (www.clem.freeserve.co.uk). He will tell you how to make some great kites from nothing but newspaper, tape, and string.

o **Leathercraft:** This is a versatile hobby. There are many different ways of working leather, each equally interesting, practical, and different to offer a variety of possibilities for the craftsperson to maintain interest for a lifetime.

o **Macramé:** With a little string, you can make belts or key rings; with a lot of string, you can make planters or wall hangings. This is another retirement hobby that you could turn into a money-spinner by calling on local retailers to make a presentation of your produce.

o **Magic:** Providing you have patience and are ready for hours of practice, you can make conjuring, popularly known as magic, a fascinating and profitable hobby. You will be in demand at children's parties and fund-raising events, and in homes and hospitals for children and adults.

o **Metalwork:** There are many metals and a number of ways of working with them. Some methods require considerable equipment and special workspace; others are possible at home with a few tools. The methods by which some or all of these metals can be worked are engraving, etching, stamping, tooling, and turning.

o **Model-making:** Model trains, ships, and planes; models of machines, both old and new; solid models; working models – the hobbyist with a yen for model-making has a hobby good for a lifetime. Visit Hobby's (www.hobby.uk.com), a recently launched website, for sundry model-making ideas. Scale Modeling Central (http://home.centurytel.net/ ~bjepsen/) is another good starting point. The website covers equipment, techniques, buying tips, and detailing at both beginner and intermediate levels. It also contains product reviews, feature articles, frequently asked questions (FAQs), and links to related websites. You might also want to visit the website of Hobbies (Dereham) Limited (www.hobbies-dereham.co.uk). The company supplies a vast range of toys and model-making equipment worldwide through the famous *Hobbies Handbook*. You can order any product from the website.

o **Mosaic art:** This is an ancient art that is once again thriving, and makes for an undemanding retirement hobby. Create designs using tiny pieces of glass, stone, clay, or seed.

o **Museums:** If you live in an area that has its own museums, consider yourself in luck. Visiting museums can be a stimulating, satisfying, and educational hobby. Whether the museums house art treasures or remnants from man's early existence, they provide something for everyone to marvel at, learn from, and enjoy.

o **Music:** Learn to play an instrument, collect or make folk instruments, attend concerts, add to your collections of records, join a chorus or orchestra, or form your own group. Music is an ideal retirement interest, because it lends itself to both solitary and social enjoyment.

o **Photography:** Photography is a hobby with legions of followers. Anyone choosing this hobby on a trial basis should beware of the possibility of lifelong addiction. Those who have been bitten by the photography bug will tell you that they suffer no pain that the taking of another picture doesn't cure.

o **Pottery:** Create something from raw earth and experiment with shape and colour. This hobby is enormously satisfying: consequently, pottery is one of the fastest-growing retirement crafts.

o **Puppeteering:** This is an unusual hobby, but very satisfying for the creative type. This website (www.mimicspro ductions.co.uk) gives details of how to design and produce your own puppets and stages in different styles, as well as providing links to related websites.

o **Radio:** Amateur radio allows millions worldwide to communicate with each other. Radio amateurs even have their own satellites and can transmit TV pictures from their own homes. The Radio Society of Great Britain (www.rsgb.org.uk) is the UK's internationally acclaimed society for all radio amateurs.

o **Reading:** Too much could never be said for reading as a hobby. The person who admits to a dull life has never really read a book. We can travel the world or be wildly adventurous right in our own armchairs. We can bring faraway things to hand or let ourselves be carried back to ages past through books. All the wisdom, beauty, knowledge, information, and inspirational thought that man has been able to put into words on a printed page can be made our own through reading. The individual with reading as a hobby holds the joy, the laughter, the beauty, the wisdom, the sorrow, and the hopes of humankind through the ages in the books they hold in their hands.

o **Sewing, knitting, crocheting, and weaving:** As pastimes, these handicrafts have the virtue of being readily started and stopped as time permits. As moneymakers, they are somewhat limited by competition.

o **Sightseeing:** Some retirees make a hobby out of travelling around from place to place to catch up on aspects of our heritage that they never had time to enjoy while they were working, for example, stately homes, listed buildings, conservation areas, churches, and cathedrals.

o **Sports:** Many people get great excitement from watching and participating in sports. You don't have to possess any physical qualifications to make it as a fan, and fortunately there are a number of moderate sports like tennis, golf, boating, fishing, and bowling that are good exercise and fun for most of us. Be careful, though, not to overdose on spectator sports.

o **Upholstering:** A beginners' class in upholstering would be a good place to start, as this hobby does require rather exact skills. Strong hands and nimble fingers are a real asset.

o **Walking:** Whether you are a long-distance hiker or a short-distance walker, the time you spend walking can be a pleasure-filled experience. Most of us could walk a little each day, and be better off physically and mentally for it.

o **Website creation:** My research tells me that website creation is rapidly growing in popularity with retirees, as is attested by 78-year-old Ron King in the case study below.

o **Winemaking:** With experience, you can attempt to reproduce in your own wines the characteristics you find most desirable in fine vintage wines. A good wine-tasting class usually precedes the interest created in this hobby.

o **Woodcarving:** You only have to visit Oberammergau to be overawed and inspired by this craft. Every child in this town is taught to carve; small wonder that it is a Mecca for woodcarvers. Don't discount woodcarving as a possible retirement hobby until you give it a fair trial.

o **Woodworking:** Here is another choice that has income-producing potential, since skilled woodworkers, carpenters, and furniture restorers are much in demand.

o **Writing:** Do you have the urge to write a novel, short stories, or poems? Perhaps you have always wanted to try your hand at journalism? The web is a major source of advice on writing and research resources. If you fancy writing mysteries, The Mystery Writers' Forum (at www.ideas4writers.co.uk/public/ideas/mystery.php) provides information on forensics, poisons, guns, and other topics that will help you get your facts right. Writing for the web itself is now a major activity and the Trace Project (www.trace.ntu.ac.uk), run by Nottingham University, focuses on online writing. There is a structured website tour to take you through the facilities, which include writing communities, competitions, conferences, and online discussions. Perhaps you are already writing and want to know more about publishing. Have a look at Dan Poynter's Para Publishing (www.parapublishing.com). This gives guidance on every aspect of publishing, including self-publishing. Maybe a course is required to develop your writing talents? The Arvon Foundation (www.arvonfoundation.or g) runs inexpensive one-week residential writing courses at inspiring locations in Devon, Yorkshire, and Scotland. The courses cover the writing of fiction, poetry, travelogue, and screenplays. As a final thought (here cometh the commercial), surf over to my own website (www.writing-for-profit.com) and make a start on learning to write niche non-fiction in retirement (Fig. 10.1).

Case study

Webmaster Ron (78) builds four hobby websites
On 21 June 2003, Ron King launched his new hobby: a multi-page website (www.grandadsez.co.uk) dedicated to older surfers (Fig. 10.2).

Fig. 10.1 The author's resource centre for writing in retirement

Fig. 10.2 One of Ron King's hobby websites

It is a fun website and, if the wry copy is anything to go by, I suspect Ron himself is a bundle of laughs. Included in the contents are articles on retirement hobbies, current affairs, finance, music, railways, and pet hates! Ron is the epitome of a retiree bursting with energy and hell-bent on getting the best out of his third-age years. Visit the website and check out the hobbies section. He has some interesting thoughts on the topic.

When I contacted Ron to secure permission for including his retirement endeavours in my book, he replied:

Thanks for this; I'm pleased to know that us old 'uns can still keep up with the times. My name is Ron King and I will be 78 years of age shortly. I'm a retired design engineer and live in a tiny flat with my wife. I find that messing about with a computer is a great hobby. It takes up little room, makes very little mess, and is quick to finish with at the end of the day. My main interest is in making websites; I have four:

www.grandadsez.co.uk
www.andoverfair.co.uk (mainly about computing)
www.king27.freeserve.co.uk (about the classic Amstrad PCW computers)
www.yamsen.org.uk (a website which I authored and maintain for YAMSEN, a Yorkshire charity).

Wow, not one but four websites ... and Ron has only just begun. He also manages to double as a volunteer for one of these websites.

Personal case study

Hobbies feature strongly in my own portfolio for enrichment, and I have several: writing, watercolour painting, and an enduring passion for researching the period of transition from silent to talking films. Currently, I am combining all three in an endeavour to produce a manuscript for an illustrated book notionally entitled *The Hollywood Revolution: 1927–9*. (Quirky, yes, I know.) To test the water, I created a 30-minute radio drama on the topic, which has been accepted by BBC Radio 4 for late-night scheduling in 2005.

Even if you have never before indulged in hobbies, think about developing an interest now in retirement. Not only is it fun, but it also stretches the mind. Only recently, I was introduced to an 86-year-old who had just taken up a hobby for the first time in his life: building scale models of vintage racing cars for his great-grandsons. He was clearly enjoying every minute of his new-found interest – and that is fulfilment.

11

Toning up for a healthy lifestyle

You are only as old as you have a mind to be, and so toning up for a healthy lifestyle in retirement makes good sense. Don't dread the advancing years; embrace them generously by keeping fit in mind and body. You will add years to your lifespan if you do.

Ageing gracefully

The ways in which we currently conceive of age have been programmed into us, and by and large we have accepted this concept as a reality. As a society, almost without exception, we have come to believe that we all will get old, sick, senile, frail, and die – in that order. This doesn't have to be true for us any longer. As we refuse to accept these old fears and beliefs, we can make this a time when we begin to reverse the negative parts of the ageing process. The current crop of baby boomers isn't going to sit back and age like their parents did. We will live longer and, if we take charge of our health, we will live exciting, productive lives.

The third age of the lifespan can be even more wonderful than the first and second ages. We can make these years exciting, if we have a mind to. If we want to age successfully, then we must make a conscious choice to do so. Healthy ageing is about learning how to keep the life force strong within us. We can do this with self-love, and with good food and exercise.

Staying healthy into our later years is an act of loving ourselves. We can:

o make deliberate choices to care for who we are;
o study books on nutrition to learn how to fuel our bodies with the most nutritious foods possible;
o explore some form of exercise to keep our bones strong and our bodies flexible;
o listen to tapes or take classes that teach us how to use our minds; and
o learn how to think in ways that support a peaceful, loving, healthy life.

Living a healthy life

Fast food and packaged processed foods don't support life, no matter how pretty and mouth-watering the pictures on the packaging. Our bodies need fresh, living foods, such as fruits, vegetables, and cereals, as well as small amounts of meat, poultry, and fish. These are the foods that will sustain our bodies well into old age. You may not want to hear this, but many nutritionists claim that 'soul food' is also 'heart attack food'. It may please the taste buds but, eaten consistently over a lifetime, it contributes to all sorts of health problems.

As teenagers we can get away with a lot of poor food choices. We may not feel our best, but at least we don't feel unwell. However, when we reach the mid-60s, our past food history begins to catch up with us. This is when so many people find that their bodies start to malfunction and diseases begin to show. Ask yourself, 'How do I want to age?' Observe people who are ageing miserably and notice those who are ageing magnificently. What do these two groups do differently? Are you willing to do what it takes to be healthy, happy, and fulfilled in your later years? The more we study what is right with older people, the more we will know how we can all accomplish healthy living.

Accepting and loving your body

It is crucial to our well-being to love and appreciate ourselves in a sustained way. Loving our bodies is important at any stage of our lives, but it is absolutely vital as we grow older. Anger isn't healing. If we put anger into any part of our bodies, especially a part that is sick, it only delays the healing process. If there is some part of your body that you aren't happy with, then take a month or so and put love into that area on a daily basis. Tell your body that you love it.

Sycophantic? Don't you believe it; it works.

What if part of your body is sagging or wrinkled? This part has been with you for a lifetime, and it is doing the best it can with the health choices you have made. Hating your body won't make it young and beautiful. Love your body, and it will love you back. Take care of your body and love every bit of it, from the top of your head to the tips of your toes – and all the organs in between. When you love yourself, others will love you too.

Our thoughts and our words shape our experiences. So we can quite unknowingly, just by thinking, contribute to our health or to our diseases. Dr Candace Pert discovered neuropeptides, the chemical messengers in our brain that travel to every part of our body, touching every cell and depositing a bit of that chemical in it. They do this each time we think a thought or speak a word. If our thoughts are fearful, angry, or in any way negative, then the chemicals these messengers deposit depress our immune systems. If our thoughts are loving, optimistic, and positive, then the different chemicals these messengers deposit will enhance our immune systems. So, moment by moment, we are consciously or unconsciously choosing healthy thoughts or unhealthy thoughts. Poisonous thoughts poison our bodies. We can't allow ourselves to indulge in negative thinking. It will make us sick and kill us.

In addition to making sound choices for ourselves nutritionally and medically, we need to take charge of our thinking. *Negative thinking produces negative experiences.* If we want to change our lives for the better, we must learn to think thoughts that support us and help improve the quality of our lives. When we love and appreciate who we are, we naturally take better care of ourselves.

Keeping fit

Having established that keeping fit starts in the mind, let us now turn our attention to ways and means to keep the body in good order.

Reconsider the meaning of fitness

The word 'fitness' conjures up all sorts of images in the mind – most connected with 20- and 30-year-olds dressed in the latest designer training gear, sweating away while they perform whatever happens to be the trendy form of workout for that month. If the very thought of any sort of fitness activity fills you with horror, think again. It needn't be a form of punishment; it can actually be enjoyable, even when you arrive at the third age.

Reconsider the value of exercise

If you don't exercise, you will find that fat displaces muscle, and muscles become smaller and weaker, in a process known as atrophy. You will also gain weight more easily, because, even at rest, muscles burn more calories than fat does. Added weight puts added stress on your heart and lungs, and on the weight-bearing joints of the hips, knees, ankles, and feet. It then becomes more difficult to get out of a chair, climb the stairs, maintain balance, and walk. Weak muscles can't protect your joints or help to provide the strength needed for balance, so you become more prone to falls. Weak muscles and frail bones limit ability to look after yourself. Without exercise, your bones, joints, and spinal column tend to become thin and porous, in a condition known as osteoporosis.

Keeping fit can help in lots of ways. If you can do half an hour's physical activity a day, you can really improve your health. When you exercise, you help to reduce fat tissue at the same time as building muscle and bone. Strong muscles help to protect your spinal column and joints, improve balance and posture, increase your mobility, and reduce the likelihood of falls and other accidents. With exercise, bones rebuild and repair themselves. Exercise can also help cut the risk of heart disease and strokes. It will stop you from feeling tired, help reduce stress, depression, and anxiety, and increase self-confidence. It will also help you control your weight (of course, this will only happen if you eat a healthy, balanced diet), prevent constipation and associated bouts of incontinence, and combat insomnia.

Don't waste your money on training equipment

Keeping fit needn't cost a lot; you don't need to go out and buy all that fancy exercise gear. Use tinned food or bags of flour or sugar as weights, and wear tights to provide resistance.

Go for a check-up if necessary

Most people don't need a check-up before they start to get fit. However, if you are overweight, very unfit, or recovering from flu or a chest infection, or if you suffer from heart disease, high blood pressure, back problems, arthritis, joint pain, or diabetes, then you must see your doctor before you start any form of exercise.

Build up exercise gradually

If you aren't used to exercising, build up the amount you do gradually. You should start with two sessions of 15 minutes per day, and steadily build up to half an hour in one go. Whatever you do, increase the time and intensity of the exercise gently. If you suffer any pain or uncomfortable stiffness, stop and try again another time. Don't hold your breath while doing any movement. Don't exercise if you have just eaten, or if you feel unwell or tired. Don't turn your head or look up at the ceiling quickly, as this can cause dizziness.

Take a walk and use the stairs

Walk a bit more briskly and use the stairs more often. A brisk walk of 30 minutes a day is one of the easiest ways of exercising. Try walking to the shops or around to a friend's house instead of getting in the car. If you aren't keen on long walks, try using the stairs instead of lifts. Should you like walking, think about joining a group or club.

Go swimming, cycling, or dancing

Swimming is another good form of exercise, and is said to be the best for all-round fitness. Because the water supports your weight, swimming is especially good if you are overweight, suffer from back trouble or arthritis, or have a disability. If you can't swim, don't be put off – most pools hold classes for adults and some offer reduced rates for retirees.

Cycling is a cheap and healthy way to keep fit. It builds up your stamina and strengthens muscles, as well as helping you to lose weight.

Why not join a dancing class? It gives you the chance to get dressed up as well. There are classes available in all types of dance.

Outsmarting forgetfulness

Concerned about loss of memory and mental acuity as you age? While your mind and memory may slow down a bit with the passing years, there is plenty you can do to keep your brain in shape. Here are some tips to help you improve your memory skills and keep your mind active and alert.

Tips for an active mind and better memory

Consider why you are forgetful

Numerous physical and emotional conditions can contribute to memory problems, including nutritional deficiencies, dehydration, depression, loneliness, and grief. Some prescription and over-the-counter medications can affect the memory. Talk with your doctor and chemist about how your overall health status may be impacting your memory, and what you can do about it.

Drink in moderation

Alcohol is a depressant, and excessive drinking damages the brain in ways that can harm your memory. Drinking is OK in moderation (one to two drinks a day) if you aren't on medications that interact with alcohol. Be sure to tell your doctor how much alcohol you drink.

Exercise to keep your mind sharp

A brisk daily walk is pleasurable, healthy exercise – good for mind, body, and spirit. If you have been sedentary or are in poor health, start out slowly and consult your doctor first.

Try some memory kick-starters

You can find hundreds of articles and books with a wide variety of exercises and activities to hone your memory skills. These techniques are used by people of all ages, who are trying to manage an ever-increasing information load. They include such tricks as repeating a person's name when you are introduced, memorising the order of spices in your kitchen, and running the gamut from A to Z when you have completely forgotten someone's first name or surname (I use this trick all the time!).

Write things down

Jot down notes while you are talking on the phone. Make lists. Write down ideas, plans, recollections, and so on. Writing things down is a bit like a double-entry accounting system. It forces your mind to register the information twice and increases the odds that you will remember it later.

Get involved

Volunteer, join a club, learn a language, socialise, read, or engage in a hobby. Do anything but sit at home brooding. If you can't seem to overcome a negative attitude and feelings of depression, get some advice from your doctor.

Learn to meditate

Many types of meditation involve focusing your attention on just one thing, such as breathing, for a period of time each day. Regular meditation practice may help you concentrate on your daily activities.

Learning to relax

Recognising tension is the first step towards dealing with it. Becoming aware of how your body feels when you are relaxed and when you are under pressure is a good start. It is likely you know what caused immediate feelings of tension – a recent argument perhaps or certain worries you may have – but sometimes, when you are under pressure on a regular basis, the causes can be more difficult to identify.

Tell-tale tension signs can be hunched shoulders, a stiff neck, an aching jaw, headaches, excessive fidgeting, nail-biting, sweating palms, or clenched fists. You may snap at others and generally feel irritable. If you experience physical symptoms such as headaches for more than three days, it is a good idea to get them checked by your doctor. Start with the root cause of the tension and, if necessary, seek help by talking things through with someone you trust. Meanwhile, try these temporary soothers.

Have a warm bath

A warm bath is great for easing muscles and helping the mind and body to relax. Try adding a few drops of aroma-therapy oil to the water to add to the soothing atmosphere. A few candles lit around the bathroom will soften the glare on your eyes.

Do deep breathing

If you need something more immediate, try to escape to a quiet place and take three long, slow, deep breaths. This is often used by yoga teachers to begin relaxation exercises, helping you to focus on nothing else but your breathing. Stretch your body, as if you are yawning, to lengthen the muscles. If you are able to lie down, tense each part of your body in turn for a few seconds – beginning with the feet, moving on to the calves, and so on – and then completely relax each part as you go. This takes about 15 minutes and should leave you feeling more refreshed and relaxed, mentally and physically.

Indulge in a massage

For those with more time on their hands, massage can be a wonderful way to wind down and address specific areas of tension like the hands, shoulders, and back. Professional masseurs are trained to target tension, but a home massage, with the help of a partner, can be pretty effective.

Participating in free online fitness courses

In addition to the foregoing on leading a healthy lifestyle, you can also participate in two valuable fitness courses, both online at www.coursepal.com and free of charge. No registration is required; you can begin these courses at any time and work at your own pace.

The challenge of being healthy

Visit www.coursepal.com/apps/go.php4?id=H4N for this course, devised by the School of Champions. The course is divided into eleven main lessons:

1 survey question
2 medical
3 diagnosis
4 specific diseases
5 diet
6 exercise
7 cleanliness
8 longevity
9 complementary medicine
10 animal health
11 resources.

Practising the presence: a course in meditation

Visit www.coursepal.com/apps/go.php4?id=NS0 for this

course, devised by Tom Pritscher. The course is divided into four main lessons:

1 eye movements and breath
2 the sound part
3 practising the presence
4 the sleep meditation.

Shaping up around the house and garden

You can shape up your mind and body simultaneously when you are devoting time to workaday jobs around the house and garden. Instead of treating these necessary activities as chores, fit them into a regular schedule that includes all the other things you *really* like to do. That way everything gels, and you eliminate the unpleasant task factor.

12

Getting the best out of travel in retirement

We all need a break now and then, but how we decide to spend these essential refreshers is a matter of personal preference. For some, it will be niche travel to exotic locations; for others, short breaks in less salubrious surroundings. And it isn't all down to champagne and beer budgeting. Some retirees with discretionary funds at their disposal opt for local holidaying, while many who are less well-heeled prefer to travel abroad, even if they have to copper up to afford it.

All-in-one guide to holiday planning

Wherever your proclivities lie, you need a plan and access to resources to get the best out of travel in retirement. You need an entrée that allows you to:

o tap into time- and cost-sensitive information;

o review options;
o make price comparisons;
o find the best deals;
o maximise on value; and
o link venues and facilities to personal preferences, such as:
  o resort holidays;
  o coach holidays;
  o self-catering in the UK;
  o self-catering in Europe and worldwide;
  o short breaks;
  o singles' holidays;
  o golfing holidays;
  o cruises; and
  o holiday weather.

This chapter is your all-in-one holiday guide, containing a compendium of links for online planning; links that will still be of value even if you decide to effect buying decisions offline. Check out the International Retirement Directory at the end of this book for additional useful listings, including hotels, flights, airports, ferries, trains, and car hire.

Resort holidays

Sunny relaxing beaches or, perhaps, shuttling the grandchildren off to Florida ... you will be spoilt for choice.

o **Advantage Travel** (www.advantage4travel.com/v2home/ holidays/index.html). Europe's biggest network of independent travel agents, with 900 outlets in the UK, offers flights, package holidays, cruises, and more.
o **Airtours** (www.uk.mytravel.com). You can check holiday and flight details, and order a brochure, online.

o **Bargain Holidays** (www.bargainholidays.co.uk). Discount and last-minute holidays are available from this website. It is easy to use and has information on guides, car hire, and weather reports.

o **Caribbean Holidays** (www.caribbean.co.uk). Specialists in holiday travel to the Caribbean. Handle reservations for over 5,000 hotels and villas on 36 Caribbean islands.

o **Co-op Travelcare** (www.travelcare.co.uk). Offers holiday and flight search and discounts.

o **Crystal Holidays** (www.crystalholidays.co.uk). This operator covers France, Jersey, the UK, and the US, as well as lake, mountain, and skiing holidays. You can order a brochure online.

o **Deckchair** (www.deckchair.com). A big database of fares and good discounted prices.

o **Drive Alive** (www.drive-alive.com). Plan and book your self-drive holiday online, submit your holiday plan, and then phone if you wish. The website also offers city breaks, stopover hotels, and resort holidays.

o **Expedia** (www.expedia.co.uk). Holiday details from the UK's top 20 travel companies, so the choice is extensive. Expedia will also find the cheapest price for wherever you want to go.

o **First Choice** (www.firstchoice.co.uk). Last-minute holidays, cheap flights, and a discount for booking online.

o **French Life** (www.frenchlife.co.uk). Create tailor-made holidays in France staying in villas or cottages.

o **Instant Holidays** (www.instant-holidays.com). Last-minute holiday bargains.

o **Kuoni** (www.kuoni.co.uk). A well-known tour operator covering exotic destinations. You can book online.

o **Lakes & Mountains Holidays** (www.lakes-mounains. co.uk). City breaks, hotels, motor homes, etc. in Europe and Canada.

o **Lunn Poly** (www.lunn-poly.co.uk). Offers holidays available in coming months, plus late availability, and a selection of cruises.

o **Magic Travel Holidays** (www.magictravelgroup.co.uk). Holidays in Spain, Portugal, France, and European cities.

o **Orient-Express Trains & Cruises** (www.orient-express. com). The world's greatest train journeys.

o **Premier Leisure Holidays** (www.premier-leisure.com). Schedule and charter flights, as well as package holidays and bargain deals.

o **Saga Holidays** (www.saga.co.uk/travel/General3/home. asp). Resort holidays, tours, cruises, short breaks, special offers, late getaways, etc.

o **Scottish Holidays** (www.scottishholidays.net). Lots of information. A good search facility for accommodation.

o **Sunstyle Holidays** (www.sunstyle.co.uk). Specialists in holidays to Florida.

o **Teletext Holidays** (www.teletext.co.uk). The online service of the TV-based teletext. It is easy and fast to use, and the prices are competitive.

o **Thomas Cook** (www.thomascook.co.uk). The website of the large holiday company that started it all.

o **Thomson Holidays** (www.thomsonholidays.co.uk). As well as the usual Thomson holidays, this website also features information on Just, their no-frills holiday packages.

o **Travelfinder** (www.travel-finder.co.uk). Travel bargains departing from the UK. The website is updated daily and is easy to use. You can look for city breaks, flights, or inclusive holidays.

o **Virgin** (www.virgin.net/travel). This website covers all kinds of holidays and has lots of information.

Coach holidays

Perhaps you don't like flying? There is still a good choice of destinations if you take a coach holiday.

o **Coach Holidays** (www.coachholidays.com). Coach holidays and coach tours, departing from England, Scotland, and Wales, at discounted prices.

o **David Urquhart Travel** (www.davidurquharttravel. co.uk). Mainly coach holidays in the UK, but expanding into Europe.

o **Gold Crest Holidays** (www.gold-crest.com). A good choice, including late deals. You can order a brochure online.

o **Leger Holidays** (www.leger.co.uk). Over 300 pick-up points throughout England and Wales. Click on the map to find your nearest one. A good choice of tours, including battlefields.

o **Shearings** (www.shearingsholidays.com). Holidays in the UK, Europe, and worldwide. The website doesn't have too much information, but there is a phone number for enquiries.

o **Skills** (www.skills.co.uk). Continental holidays, plus days out. Some discounts.

o **Supreme Travel** (www.supremetravel.co.uk). A long-established, family-run company with tours covering continental Europe and the UK.

o **Titan Travel** (www.titantravel.co.uk). A large tour operator offering escorted holidays all over the world.

o **Wallace Arnold** (www.wallacearnold.com). An extensive choice of destinations. You can view holidays or order a brochure online.

o **Wise Coaches** (www.wisecoaches.co.uk). Hassle-free holidays and short breaks throughout the UK, plus Ireland, France, Belgium, and the Netherlands. A free door-to-door service from East Sussex. Tours include all coach travel and holiday insurance, plus most include evening meals and bed and breakfast.

o **Woods** (www.woodstravel.co.uk). Holidays throughout Europe and the UK. A free door-to-door service between Eastbourne and Southampton, and up to 30 miles inland. On certain holidays, the company can arrange to pick up clients from most areas of the country, collecting you from home in a taxi.

Self-catering in the UK

Holiday cottages to Scottish castles, all situated in the best UK locations.

o **Cottageguide** (www.cottageguide.co.uk). A selection of over 3,000 self-catering holiday homes, including farmhouses, country houses, town houses, apartments, and log cabins.

o **Cumbrian Cottages** (www.cumbria-cottages.co.uk). All of the holiday homes have been personally selected and are also inspected by the English Tourism Council.

o **Dales Holiday Cottages** (www.dales-holiday-cottages.com). A range of cottages in Yorkshire, Northumberland, the Lake District, and Scotland. Check availability and book online.

o **Ecosse Unique** (www.uniquescotland.com). Cottages to rent throughout Scotland. The website features an easy-to-use map to click on for the area that you want to visit. Good pictures and descriptions for each property.

o **Hideaways** (www.hideaways.co.uk). Specialists in cottages throughout central and southern England. The website has good photographs of each property, together with descriptions and details of nearby facilities. The price is shown on the same page as the property.

o **Internet Directory of UK Holiday Accommodation** (www.holidays.org.uk). This website has a vast number of holidays to choose from, including self-catering. Just type in the town you want to visit, choose by county, or click on the map.

o **Northern Ireland Self Catering Holidays Association** (www.nischa.com). A guide to over 350 holiday homes, cottages, and holiday rentals in Northern Ireland.

o **Red Rose Cottages** (www.redrosecottages.co.uk). This website has cottages, apartments, and houses to rent in the north of England. Good pictures of the properties, together with accompanying descriptions. The price is shown on the same page as the property, along with classification from the English Tourist Board.

o **Scottish Holiday Cottages** (www.scottish-holiday-cottages.co.uk). Holiday accommodation to rent in locations throughout Scotland, from the Borders to the Highlands.

o **UK Holiday Cottages Online** (www.oas.co.uk/uk cottages). Cottages and self-catering accommodation throughout the UK.

o **Vivat Trust** (www.vivat.org.uk). Vivat is a non-profit organisation dedicated to preserving unusual ancient buildings and offering them as rented accommodation. The trust has cottages, houses, and apartments, all with furnishings appropriate to the period. The website has good pictures of the properties, together with comprehensive descriptions.

o **Wales Holiday Cottages** (www.wales-holidays.co.uk). An easy-to-use website with a very good selection of cottages to rent in Wales.

Self-catering in Europe and worldwide

Villas, gîtes, apartments ... Find a holiday home that is right for you.

Canary Islands

o **Island Accommodation** (www.islandaccommodation. com). Luxury villas and self-catering apartments in Lanzarote, Fuerteventura, Gran Canaria, Tenerife, and Gomera.

o **Sunseeker Holidays** (www.sunseekerholidays.com). Specialists in holiday accommodation on Fuerteventura. They really do know the best places to stay (as well as the places to avoid).

Caribbean

o **Country Villas** (www.countryvillas.com) A selection of superb villas on the Caribbean islands of Barbados, St Lucia, and Mustique. The size of accommodation varies from two to six bedrooms, giving something for everyone.

o **Eden Holidays** (www.edenholidays.com). Holiday villa rentals on the Caribbean islands of Jamaica, Tobago, and Grenada.

Cyprus

o **Owners Direct** (www.ownersdirect.co.uk/cyprus.htm). Villas and apartments in Cyprus. Self-catering holiday accommodation. Book direct with the owners.
o **Villa Villas** (www.villavillas.com). Good selection of villas. The website shows prices and availability.

France

o **Cote d'Azur Villas** (www.cotedazurvillas.co.uk). A wide choice of exclusive villas, all with pools, in the Côte d'Azur region of southern France.
o **Normandie Vacances** (www.normandy-holidays.co.uk). Established in 1982, the only UK specialist tour operator for one of the finest holiday regions in France. Offers over 120 self-catering country cottages and houses, all with Gîtes de France classification. Over half are within 30 minutes' drive of the sea.

Greece

o **Elysian Holidays** (www.elysianholidays.com). An extensive choice of properties on Greek islands, with information about each island.
o **Travelux** (www.mainland-greece-and-greek-island-holidays. co.uk/index.shtml). Apartments and villas with pools on the Ionian Islands and in mainland Greece.

Italy

o **Italian Holidays** (www.italianholidays.co.uk/). Superb holiday rentals and properties in charming and traditional country houses, farmhouses, and villas in all the most beautiful regions of Italy.

o **Italian Villas** (www.villavillas.com). A wide selection of villas and apartments in Italy, ranging from studio apartments for two people to large villas and farmhouses, with private pools set in wonderful locations, accommodating up to 16 and more people.

Portugal

o **Individual Travellers** (www.indiv-travellers.com). Properties throughout Portugal.
o **Villa Agency** (www.thevillaagency.co.uk). Villas with pools to rent in the Algarve and coastal region of Lisbon.

Spain

o **Villa Plus** (www.villapluscostadelsol.com/). A specialist in the Costa del Sol, this operator has been arranging villa holidays since 1986.
o **Experience Spain** (www.expspain.com). Self-catering apartments and villas available for holiday rental, located in some of the most desirable areas of Andalusia, the Costa del Sol, and southern Spain.

US

o **Bridgewater Villa** (www.bridgewatervilla.co.uk). A holiday home in Florida. Sleeps eight to ten. Four bedrooms and three bathrooms. A south-facing luxury villa with pool, on the private development of Bridgewater Crossing. Ideally located for all the main attractions.
o **Windsor Palms** (www.travel55.co.uk/breda_windsor palms.html). Another holiday home in Florida, this time in Kissimmee, Orlando. Sleeps ten. Four bedrooms and three bathrooms. A luxury villa with pool, within five minutes' drive of Disney World. Gold Star rating.

Short breaks

We all need to recharge our batteries – what better than a weekend away?

o **Crystal Holidays** (www.crystalholidays.co.uk). City breaks are available with this company. You can order a brochure online.

o **En Route** (www.enroute.co.uk). City breaks throughout the UK and continental Europe, as well as further afield.

o **Hire Boats2Go** (www.hireboats2go.co.uk). Boats are normally available for three-night weekend breaks from Friday to Monday or four-night midweek breaks from Monday to Friday.

o **Inntravel** (www.inntravel.co.uk). Short breaks available throughout Europe. An attractive, easy-to-use website.

o **Rose Narrowboats** (www.roseboat.demon.co.uk). This is a very attractive website, which gives lots of information about boats for hire, with good pictures and descriptions. Some boats are available for short breaks.

o **Short Break Holidays** (www.travel-quest.co.uk/tqweekend. htm). Includes details on *Classic Short Breaks in Europe*, a book published by Thomas Cook Publishing in association with Classic FM that suggests over 100 places in which to enjoy a short break holiday.

o **Superbreak** (www.superbreaks.com). Instant reservations at over 1,500 hotels throughout the UK and Europe.

o **Travelgate** (www.travelgate.co.uk). A short-break holiday directory.

o **Warner** (www.warnerholidays.co.uk). Specialises in UK short breaks for adults.

o **Web Weekends** (www.webweekends.co.uk). Weekend breaks on offer all year round in the UK and abroad.

o **White Roc** (www.whiteroc.co.uk). Skiing weekends, or any number of skiing days, from November to May.

Singles' holidays

A few operators offer singles' holidays with no supplements. Unless stated otherwise, the operators below do charge supplements for singles' holidays.

o **Friendship Travel** (www.friendshiptravel.co.uk). Holidays to Greece and Turkey for independent single travellers. Some prices are for single rooms, others for twin rooms. Check which you are being quoted for.

o **Holiday Encounters** (www.singles-holidays.co.uk). Package holidays catering for single people who like to holiday to exotic locations in the company of others.

o **Singles Friendly** (www.singlesfriendly.co.uk). Hotel and bed-and-breakfast accommodation in England, Scotland, and Wales.

o **Solitair** (www.solitairhols.com). A good choice of destinations and activities. No singles' supplement.

o **Solo's Holidays** (www.solosholidays.co.uk). An extensive choice of holidays in the UK and overseas, including exotic destinations, golfing holidays, and cruises. This website is worth a look.

o **Spanish Activity Breaks** (www.spanishactivitybreaks.co.uk). A limited choice of dates with this company on their Spanish holidays.

o **TrekAmerica** (www.trekamerica.co.uk/). Offers activity holidays, adventure travel and singles holidays in the national parks of the USA, Canada, Alaska and Mexico.

Golfing holidays

Golfing holidays the world over. Or play the most famous in the home of golf – Scotland.

o **Course Master** (www.golfholidaysonline.com). Golfing holidays to Portugal, Spain, Scotland, Canada, Morocco, and Florida.

o **Dubai Golf Holidays** (www.dubai-holidays4less.co.uk). Golfing holiday packages at the Emirates Golf Club and the Dubai Creek Golf and Yacht Club.

o **Golfbreaks** (www.golfbreaks.com). Short golfing breaks throughout the UK.

o **Golf Holidays in France** (www.frenchgolfholidays.com). The home of great golfing holidays in France.

o **Golf in the Sun** (www.golfinthesun.co.uk). Destinations include Spain, Portugal, Lisbon, Tenerife, Tunisia, Cyprus, France, and Majorca. A choice of over 100 golf courses. Accommodation ranges from self-catering apartments to four- and five-star hotels.

o **Golf Scotland** (www.golfscotland.co.uk). Choose from one of three tours – Legends, Deluxe Legends, or Classic Treasures – or have a tailor-made package to suit your individual requirements. The operator has extensive experience and first-hand knowledge of areas, courses, and hotels.

o **Irish Caddy** (www.irishcaddy.com). A great-looking website, which is easy to use and provides a golfing experience custom-made to your needs, no matter what level of golf you play.

o **Long Shot** (www.longshotgolf.co.uk). A large but easy-to-use website. Golf the world over. Twenty-seven years' experience.

o **Myrtle Beach Golf Holidays** (www.golfholiday.com). Ninety-six golf courses in the Myrtle Beach area featured on this website. Book courses and accommodation online.

o **Scotland Golf Tours** (www.scotland-golf-tours.co.uk). Golfers are offered a collection of travel packages to Scotland, arranged by Scottish golfers.

o **Tailor Made Golf** (www.tailormadegolf.co.uk). Golfing holidays in Tenerife, Costa del Sol, Portugal, Jersey, South Africa, and the US.

o **Welsh Golfing Holidays** (www.welshgolfingholidays. co.uk). A wide range of golf courses, of varying degrees of difficulty to suit different standards of golfers. Accommodation and course booking are included.

Cruises

Out of favour for many years, cruises are now one of the most popular holiday choices for the over-50s.

o **Alaska CruiseTour** (www.atlastravelweb.com/). River cruising, small ship cruising; cruises around Australia and the South Pacific, Canada and New England, and Hawaii.

o **Chancery Cruising** (www.holborn-travel.co.uk). Discount cruises and theme-music cruises.

o **Check-in Cruises** (www.check-in-cruises.co.uk). Specialists in cruises to the Caribbean, Bermuda, the Panama Canal, and Alaska. Direct deals with cruise lines and airlines to offer discounts.

o **Cruise Control** (www.cruisecontrolcruises.co.uk). This independent agent offers a wide range of discount cruises from all the leading cruise lines. Search the database or view the special offers and late deals.

o **The Cruise Shop** (www.thecruiseshop.co.uk). This website says they will 'beat a quote' that you have already been given for a cruise. If you email your request, they will get back to you within 24 hours.

o **Cruise Services** (www.cruiseservices.co.uk). A good choice of destinations. You can search by the name of the destination or ship.

o **Fred Olsen Cruise Lines** (www.fredolsencruises.co.uk). One of the top cruise lines – an award winner in 2000. An attractive, easy-to-use website, with a good choice of destinations.

o **P & O** (www.pocruises.com). An extensive choice of cruises throughout the world. The website takes a while to get into, as there are quite a few links, but once you have decided on a cruise you like the look of, you will find a decent description.

o **Page & Moy** (www.cruisecollection.com). An attractive, easy-to-use website, with details of destinations, ships, dates, and prices.

o **Scantours** (www.scantoursuk.com). Specialists in cruises to Russia and five Scandinavian countries. The website is easy to use and the choice is quite extensive.

o **Sealand Travel** (www.sealandtravel.com). In addition to the usual choice of cruise lines and destinations, the website features a special section on singles' cruising.

o **Seaview** (www.seaview.co.uk). A good-looking website, which gives lots of information and up-to-date news on all aspects of cruises. An extensive list of cruise operators.

Holiday weather

Don't let the weather spoil your holiday. Visit www.uknet
guide.co.uk/ to check out the holiday weather.

13

Monitoring progress using an audit checklist

You have been using checklists as an aid to accomplishment all your life, and you will continue to tick away at them in retirement. Now you are about to complete one of the most important checklists you will ever tackle: your own personal audit checklist for third-age fulfilment. You have covered the basics and reviewed some recognised options for implementation. Now make a start on putting the precepts into position at the starting gate of your masterplan. Use the example below as a benchmark for evaluating the elements that will make for happiness and success in *your* retirement. The audit checklist will provide you with the essentials for conducting a comprehensive search to locate existing or potential areas for improvement, and for addressing opportunities as they arise.

This instrument isn't exhaustive, that is, you must rely on personal judgement and preferences. However, it does provide a systematic framework to ensure that critical areas have been addressed before action is taken. The audit is a tool, not a replacement for sound reasoning. Audits can't ensure a happy and successful retirement. However, effectively designed instruments such as this can save valuable time in monitoring progress in your quest to plan ahead for fulfilment in the third age.

How to use the audit for maximum effectiveness

o *Answer all questions 'yes' or 'no,'* with an affirmative indicating action underway or a negative indicating action still under consideration in a specific area.
o *Review your own analysis* of each section to determine progress, and then keep referring back. Regular use of this audit instrument will help to make you more efficient in planning ahead for fulfilment in the third age.

1 *The secret of the three little boxes*

1 Are you coming to terms with the new concept of retirement?
2 Are you preparing for your transition into third-age beginnings?
3 Are you determined to squeeze every ounce of potential out of your retirement years?
4 Do you now realise why third-age people form a unique group?
5 Do you accept that age alone isn't a criterion for a successful retirement?
6 Will you embrace your new lifestyle generously?
7 Will you give the thumbs down to popular myths about retirement?

8 Will you make a start on putting your plans into position?

9 Can you now appreciate why enjoying a fulfilling and enriching third age exceeds the wildest expectations of youth?

2 The keys to a happy and successful retirement

1 Have you thought about what will you need to enjoy the retirement years?

2 Can you envisage what the future will hold?

3 Are you giving attention to financial planning?

4 Are you estimating how much you should save towards your retirement?

5 Do you know how to establish the guidelines on saving?

6 Are you confident you can compensate for the loss of job-related benefits?

7 Can you identify the general keys to a happy and successful retirement?

8 Can you identify the specific keys to a happy and successful retirement?

3 Setting the goals for your new way of life

1 Have you mastered the steps and stairs to goal-setting?

2 Can you clarify your objectives for ensuring a happy and successful retirement?

3 Have you contemplated expanding your education?

4 Have you embraced new technology?

5 Have you considered working part-time?

6 Have you thought about starting your own business?

7 Can you see how others will benefit if you pass on your knowledge?

8 Have you considered developing new hobbies?

9 Have you contemplated doing voluntary work?

10 Do you think that travel will broaden your perspective?

11 Will you take measures to instigate a personal fitness regime?

12 Will you cultivate your sense of humour?

13 Will you undertake to think positively about the future?

4 Learning something new

1 Do you agree that the more you learn in retirement, the more you are likely to increase your fulfilment?

2 Have you enquired yet about adult learning in your own community?

3 Have you taken time out to discover the largest e-learning network in the UK?

4 Do you appreciate that you will never know what learning can do for you unless you try?

5 Do you know your way around the maze of courses available online?

6 Do you accept that if 70- and 80-year-olds can acquire computer skills, so can you?

7 Have you asked at your local public library about the People's Network?

8 Have you thought about tackling a degree course at the University of the Third Age?

9 Have you considered running a business at home using distance learning?

10 Have you enquired whether you might be eligible for financial help as an adult learner?

5 *Getting up to speed in cyberspace*

1 Will you master email to keep in touch with family and friends everywhere?

2 Will you learn how to create websites for fun or profit, or both?

3 Will you take the trouble to discover little-known sources of free information?

4 Will you consider planning holidays online before you commit to expenditure?

5 Will you trace your ancestry online?

6 Will you use the internet to locate lost friends and make new friends online?

7 Will you go online to find hobbies to add spice to your retirement?

8 Will you go window-shopping online to compare prices before buying offline?

9 Have you registered at the website dedicated to free third-age learning?

10 Have you visited the portals for retirees?

11 Have you studied the range of third-age projects with the retirees' search facilities?

12 Will you consider posting messages on bulletin boards?

13 Will you join discussion forums?

14 Will you make use of seniors' discount malls?

6 *Keeping your hand in part-time*

1 Do you know you can still pick up your state pension when you work part-time?

2 Do you have a special skill that has never been put to the test?

3 Have you taken a trip on the Worktrain to review your options?

4 Have you made enquiries to ascertain whether New Deal 50 plus might benefit you financially?

7 Starting a business for fun or profit

1 Will you follow in the footsteps of countless other retirees who derive satisfaction from running a business in retirement?

2 Will you use your powers of self-reflection to find ideas?

3 Have you checked what businesses other retirees are running successfully?

4 Do you know how to fine-tune the evaluation process before leaping in?

5 Do you know how to evaluate any business proposition?

6 Will you undertake research to iron out any wrinkles?

7 Will you spend time cultivating start-up prowess through professional online training at no expense?

8 Will you add to your business skills by following an offline training programme provided by the public sector?

9 Will you consider setting up an internet business at home?

10 How will you exercise prudence in selecting a trading name?

11 Can you create a masterful business plan?

12 Do you know the best place to start when shopping for seed money?

8 Participating in voluntary work

1 Are you aware that you can do voluntary work at any age?

2 Do you appreciate that your skills and experience will make a real difference to the community?

3 Have you enquired yet about the Retired and Senior Volunteer Programme?

4 Are you prepared to reach out to others less fortunate and achieve personal fulfilment?

5 Have you thought about enlisting with the Experience Corps?

9 Writing up your experiences to benefit others

1 Are you facing up to mental blocks that may be bugging you?

2 Do you reckon you lack creativity?

3 Have you tried again and again without success?

4 Given any perceived shortfalls, how will test your aptitude for writing non-fiction?

5 Can you benefit from introspection in writing self-help literature?

6 Will you consider writing a book?

7 Will you consider creating a dedicated website?

8 Will you consider writing as a memento for your grandchildren?

10 Taking the hobby route to self-actualisation

1 Do you think a suitable hobby will compensate for losing the benefits of work?

2 Can you afford the hobby?

3 Are you physically able to become involved?

4 Do you have enough room at home to accommodate the hobby?

5 Does the hobby allow you to retain your privacy?

6 Does the hobby provide opportunities to work with others?

7 Do you really have time for the hobby?

8 Can you develop the necessary skill to do the hobby?

9 Will you carefully consider all the options before you select a hobby?

11 Toning up for a healthy lifestyle

1 Will you determine to age gracefully?

2 Do you have plans in place to live a healthy life?

3 Will you learn how to accept and love your body just as it is?

4 Will you set up a regime for keeping fit in mind and body?

5 Will you master the techniques for outsmarting forgetfulness?

6 Will you learn how to relax?

7 Will you keep in shape around the house and garden?

12 Getting the best out of travel in retirement

1 Can you afford to travel around the world?

2 Will you settle for short-hop local holidays?

3 Have you investigated what holidays are on offer?

4 Do you know where to find the best deals at home and abroad?

Seize the day

Yesterday is history, tomorrow a mystery, so concentrate on the only time you ever have: *now*. This audit checklist is the gateway to your masterplan for fulfilment in retirement (coming up next).

14

Devising the masterplan that keeps on evolving

Actualising your lifetime goals in retirement doesn't just happen. You need a plan, a special plan: a *masterplan*. Some misguided optimists settle for the standard kit – jot down a few sketchy goals, cobble up a hobby or two, wrap it all up in a snazzy folder – and file it. Such a mundane plan will not suffice, if you are to ensure a happy and successful retirement. At the outset it can be as modest as a single sheet of A4, because it will grow and evolve in time, as you lay down new and essential parameters to guide you on your journey of enrichment in the third age. It will of course contain the usual nuts and bolts, but it will also include something of more intrinsic value. This masterplan will highlight your own personal philosophy on your retirement, how you will shape your activities and how you will actualise your goals in tandem with your aspirations. You will live, eat, and sleep with your masterplan for most of your retirement years. It will become your personal bible but, unlike the Bible, it won't be written in tablets of stone; it will be forever changing, forever growing, forever evolving.

Getting your creative juices flowing

Make a start on your masterplan *before* you settle on a definitive list of preferred activities. It will get the creative juices flowing and keep your mind focused on the ultimate goal. Inspiration will surge to the top in your deliberations. Any plan, be it for survival, business expansion, or ensuring a rewarding retirement, calls for a high degree of introspection. As you progress, you will find yourself facing up to reality quite readily. It is a universal truth that when you start committing your thoughts to paper, the good, the bad, and the ugly come to light fairly quickly. This can prove unsettling at first, but you will rapidly discover that you are addressing negative factors with increasing confidence and vigour. Certain aspects will call for an immediate rethink, further research, or perhaps total rejection. Now is the time to find out and put matters right. This is what will make your masterplan a winner: examining, questioning, honing, and polishing all of the elements before you fix them firmly into place. As the late Napoleon Hill, self-help author and one of the most successful US insurance brokers of his time, famously said, 'What the mind can conceive and believe, it can achieve.'

Conceiving a plan

The plan you will conceive is your blueprint for a happy and successful retirement. Plans are great things. They show you where you are going, what to do, and how to do it when you get there. Make no mistake, though; you aren't creating this plan just to get you started. It is going to be around for a long time, and you will want to review and update it regularly to take account of twists and turns along the way. That is the beauty of it. When you have a plan, you can legislate for change. Without one, you can't; you will be like the explorer in the jungle without a map.

Creating a personal checklist

While no two plans are alike, they are all based on the same premise and have similarities in structure. You did some preparation in the previous chapter and, with these initial audit findings to hand, you are now ready to create a personal checklist that will identify specific elements and slot them into position. As an additional aid to execution, we will encapsulate the core findings in this book and once again ask for answers to pertinent questions as they affect your particular deliberations. Don't be tempted to skip this exercise. Revisiting old ground will focus your attention on the core options before you shape the essential route map for third-age enrichment.

The keys to a happy and successful retirement

Understanding the general and specific keys to a happy and successful retirement is of prime importance. Interlacing specific keys with goals is of equal significance. There is little point in expanding your education, taking up part-time work, starting a business, doing voluntary work, or engaging in hobbies if all you are doing is filling in time. There must be a purpose to it. Identify the purpose and determine how it will add to the quality of your life in retirement.

o What do I really need to enjoy life in the third age?

o What will the future hold for me?

o Have I given sufficient attention to organising my finances?

o How can I diminish the disadvantages of retirement?

o Have I grasped the general keys to a happy and successful retirement?

o Do I appreciate the significance specific keys will play in my planning?

Refer back to Chapter 2 for refreshment.

Setting the goals for your new way of life

Setting your goals, and hence your plan of action, hinges upon how you decide to mix and match the activities inherent in the three little boxes of life. Don't flounder, don't leave goal-setting to someone else: make your own choices and stick with them.

o Are you aware of the prescribed steps and stairs to goal-setting?

o Can you clarify your objectives?

o Are you prepared to expand your education?

o Will you embrace new technology?

o Will you consider working part-time?

o Will you think about starting your own business?

o Can you pass on your knowledge?

o Will developing new hobbies add quality to your third-age years?

o Will you consider doing voluntary work?

o Do you want to travel and broaden your perspective?

o Can you instigate a personal fitness regime?

o Will you determine to cultivate your sense of humour?

o Are you a positive thinker?

Refer back to Chapter 3 for refreshment.

Learning something new

Don't leave education behind in the second box as you enter the third. Take it with you and keep expanding it. The more you learn in retirement the more you will enhance your lifespan, because learning not only stretches the mind but it also refreshes every sinew in the body. Refuse to be numbered among those retirees who shy away from IT under the mistaken impression that mastering the beast will prove too difficult. Nothing could be further from the truth, so get cracking, join in, and add a new dimension to your experience of the third age.

o What do you know about education facilities in your community?

o Where can you find the largest e-learning network in the UK?

o How do you contact the learndirect national learning advice line?

o Is there a UK online centre near you?

o What do you know about the People's Network?

o Have you heard of the University of the Third Age?

o Can you obtain a degree like the 90-year-old in Chapter 4?

o How can you find out whether you qualify for financial help with learning?

Refer back to Chapter 4 for refreshment.

Getting up to speed in cyberspace

There is so much you can do to enrich your retirement when you take time out to investigate the possibilities. It is easy, because the internet abounds with free online courses and learning materials, now that you know where to look.

o Will you take time out to surf the web?
o Does mastering email to keep in touch with friends appeal to you?
o How about creating your own website?
o Will you add to your expertise by learning new skills online?
o How about planning holidays online?
o Will tracing your ancestry on the internet prove a useful project?
o How about locating a few lost friends online?
o How about making new friends on the web?
o Have you thought about researching your favourite topics online?
o Can you find an interesting or unusual hobby on the internet?
o How about some cyberspace window-shopping?
o Have you ever considered comparing prices online before you buy offline?
o Will you benefit from membership of one of the third-age portals?

Refer back to Chapter 5 for refreshment.

Keeping your hand in part-time

In order to eliminate the numbing void that can be experienced on retiring from full-time work, you might think about taking up part-time work. Consider the following questions about becoming involved in part-time work.

o Do you know that you can continue to work after retirement and still pick up your state pension?
o Why not give some thought to what you might like to work at part-time?
o Will it be similar to what you did for a living?
o Will it be something in an entirely different line?
o Have you considered a trip on the Worktrain to compare options?
o Are you aware that you can benefit from New Deal 50 plus as a retiree?

Refer back to Chapter 6 for refreshment.

Starting a business for fun or profit

Deciding to become a third-age entrepreneur isn't only a rewarding and self-fulfilling experience, it is also tremendous *fun*, whether you do it for pleasure or for profit. Maybe in the past you thought about starting your own business, but wavered because the risks were too great. This time it is different because your existence won't depend on success or failure; this time, if you go ahead, you will be treating it as an exercise to add flavour and variety to your retirement.

o Do you have a hobby that you can transform into a business?
o Were you good at what you did for a living?
o Did you enjoy it?
o Can you do it again successfully without supervision?

o Are there aspects of the work you could have improved upon, if only someone had asked for your advice?

o Did the business make regular profits for your employer?

o Is there still a demand for the product or service?

o Does it lend itself to part-time entrepreneurial involvement?

o Do you want to tackle something entirely different?

o Is there any business run by other retirees that inspires you?

o Do you know where to go to find other ideas?

o Will you do some research to iron out the wrinkles?

o How can you add to your business skills?

o Will you consider starting an internet business at home?

o Do you know where to get seed funding?

o How will you go about choosing a trading name?

o Can you create a viable business plan?

Refer back to Chapter 7 for refreshment.

Participating in voluntary work

You can do voluntary work at any age. Even if you give just an hour or two a week, you can make a real difference. With time on your hands in retirement, your skills and experience can be the key to unlocking opportunity for other people less fortunate than yourself, and provide you with a real sense of purpose and achievement.

o What questions should you ask yourself before volunteering?

o What questions should you ask volunteer organisers?

o What do you know about the Retired and Senior Volunteer Programme?

o Are you prepared to reach out to others less fortunate than yourself?

o Will you enlist with the Experience Corps?

o Do you know how to set about locating voluntary organisations in your area?

Refer back to Chapter 8 for refreshment.

Writing up your experiences to benefit others

You may have considered writing up your experiences, but never got around to doing anything about it. There is plenty of help available with regard to structuring your thoughts as the subject matter for a book, website, or other medium.

o Do you know that everyone has at least one good book in them?

o Do you know what stops them writing it?

o Do you know how to test your aptitude for writing non-fiction?

o Do you know what part introspection plays in the process?

o Do you know that passing on knowledge can benefit others?

o Will you do so as a memento for your grandchildren?

o Will you consider creating a dedicated website to house your wisdom?

Refer back to Chapter 9 for refreshment.

Taking the hobby route to self-actualisation

It is good practice to have at least one hobby in retirement but better to have two, because then when your interest in one temporarily wanes, you can always switch to the other for refreshment. Some retirees would appear to focus most of their energies in this direction and, in so doing, take the hobby route to self-fulfilment. Always remember: only you can devise the masterplan for enactment. If hobbies take centre stage, so be it. It is your retirement and your life.

- o Do you know how to match a hobby to your needs?
- o Have you reread the 'Review of more than 50 popular retirement hobbies'?

Refer back to Chapter 10 for refreshment.

Constructing a blueprint

Here is where you crystallise your thoughts. There is nothing more sobering than laying them all out in front of you on sheets of virgin white paper. Imagine the overall blueprint as the trunk of a pine tree with the bold headings as branches and the bullet points as needles. If all you produce is a single page, that is OK – you will be adding more later.

Finances

- o Prepare an overview of your current net worth.
- o Ask your financial adviser for objective advice about the ways you can increase your net worth to achieve an acceptable income during your retirement years.
- o Consider other ways to add to your income, for example, part-time work or self-employment, creating streams of ancillary earnings, starting a business in retirement, or converting a hobby into a profitable pursuit.

Objectives

o This is your mission statement, and only you know how to construct it.

o Think long and hard about what constitutes the ideal retirement for you. Maybe it will be all or most of the activities we have already identified; maybe it will be a selected handful; maybe you will come up with alternatives; or maybe you will focus your energies on just one activity, and dabble in others?

o Whatever you decide is OK. It is your life, your third age, so make the most of it.

Third-age education

o Determine any shortcomings in your education that you wish to rectify.

o Are you prepared to settle for general courses?

o Will you go the whole hog and try for a third-age degree?

o Investigate government-sponsored options, such as learndirect, UK online centres, the People's Network, and the University of the Third Age.

o Decide which will best suit your purpose.

o Budget for any costs you might incur, for example, books or computer software.

Online learning

o If you don't already own a computer, think about investing in one.

o If you can't afford one, use the free service at your local public library.

o If you require initial training, take advantage of a free course available (www.EdSurf.net).

o Decide on the aspects you wish to explore.

o Review the online learning facilities listed in Chapter 5.

Part-time work

o Are you sufficiently fit to work part-time?

o Do you really need the extra income?

o Investigate the government schemes for locating part-time work.

o Is there something specific you wish to try your hand at?

o Make up a list of possibilities.

o Go for it, or not, as the case may be.

A retirement business

o Is this really for you?

o Can you afford to invest?

o If so, decide whether you will do it for fun or profit, or both.

o Come up with some viable ideas.

o Plan your research, whether on the internet, in a public reference library, or in trade journals.

o Find out about local business training courses, preferably free of charge.

o Prepare a budget.

o Ask public-sector sources about start-up grants.

o Read up on marketing techniques.

o Get cracking on your strategy.

Voluntary work

o Are you totally committed to helping others?

o Do you have the time?

o Are you sufficiently fit?

o Investigate all local volunteer activities.

o Decide where your skills lie.

o Decide where they can best be put to use.

o Can you do what Ron King did, and create a website to help out?

o Make a personal commitment that you won't jump in and then jump back out again when something more interesting comes along.

Knowledge

o Evaluate your accumulated wisdom.

o Establish the value of passing it on to others.

o Think about laying it all out in book form.

o Bring yourself up to speed on niche non-fiction writing techniques at my website (www.writing-for-profit.com).

o Think about creating a website to house your expertise.

o Devise an online newsletter for like-minded enthusiasts.

o Include a message board where they can post questions or viewpoints.

Hobbies

o List any hobbies you have that you wish to take with you into retirement.

o Can you afford these hobbies?

o Do you have room for them?

o Alternatively, if you apply yourself, can you make money out of any of them?

o If you have no hobbies, reread the 'Review of more than 50 popular retirement hobbies' in Chapter 10 and select one or two of interest.

o Can you convert any of these into money-making opportunities?

o Do you prefer hobbies that are just for fun?

SWOT analysis

o Take time out now to do some SWOT (strengths, weaknesses, opportunities, threats) analysis, and review your thinking so far.

o OK, you aren't producing a plan for business purposes upon which your entire security depends, but you *are* laying down parameters to pave the way for a happy and successful retirement. Treat this as a not-too-critical path analysis and look at where it is all leading up to. Maybe you are taking on too much, maybe not enough; only you know.

o There is nothing set in concrete, and there never will be, so make any adjustments you see fit and come back to your plan later.

Personal fitness

o Will your exercise take the form of regular walks, swimming, golf, gardening, community fitness programmes, or what?

o Above all, keep your mind in good order.

Travel

o Jot down a few thoughts on whether you think travel will feature strongly in your third-age planning. Travel is important for some retirees, but not for others.

Attitudinal approach

o Think seriously about your attitude to retirement and keep it positive, even bullish on occasion.

Notes

o Use this section to contain your working notes, articles, leaflets, brochures, and the like that you pick up along the way in preparation for your great new adventure.

Postscript

You haven't finished yet; your plan is still evolving, as you will discover in the next and final chapter ...

Case study

Lucky Jim (60) retires early and makes a million

For someone who went through life unable to read or write, my Uncle Jim did OK for himself. At the tender age of 17, and after a year of trudging around the houses in all weathers selling fruit and vegetables from a rusty old barrow, he opened his first grocery store, then another, and another, until his empire had grown to 43 such emporiums. On attaining his 60th birthday, he opted for early retirement (60 was early in those days), sold out to a conglomerate, and pocketed in excess of £1 million. Lucky Jim.

Points to note about the old darling: although illiterate, he was an instinctive mathematician; he sought no one's counsel but his own; and he was always planning something or other. Among these plans was one for early retirement which, he confided in me many years later, he made a start on the day his father lent him 15 old shillings to purchase his first stock of highly perishable comestibles ...

Personal case study

The whole pattern of my life has been shaped on the principle of planning. From the age of 12, when I decided I wanted to be published (and, a year later, reading one of my essays in the French daily newspaper *Le Jour*), through success in business, to success in retirement. It is all there for you, if you plan for it in advance. Make planning a priority for the actualisation of your goals in retirement. You won't be disappointed, because the best is yet to come.

15

Keeping right on in the third-age years

No one goes on forever, that is for sure, so it behoves us to make the very best of every moment of what is left of the rest of our lives. As Sir Harry Lauder sang to audiences around the world:

> Keep right on to the end of the road, keep right on to the end.
> Tho' the way be long, let your heart be strong, keep right on round the bend.
> Tho' you're tired and weary, still journey on, till you come to your happy abode,
> Where all you love you have been dreaming of will be there at the end of the road.

Maudlin, perhaps, but it sums the situation up nicely.

Creating your own retirement success profile

Here is something you can do to ensure that you are heading in the right direction as you keep right on to the end of the road. Subject your plan of enactment to a retirement success profile. To do this, visit www.retirementoptions.com (Fig. 15.1) and click on 'Your Retirement Options'. There you will learn how you can undertake the profile and so put your exclusive plan to the test.

There are 15 retirement success factors involved in this exercise.

1 Career reorientation: Let go.
2 Retirement value: Reframe your attitudes.
3 Personal empowerment: Take charge.

Fig. 15.1 Creating a retirement success profile

4 Physical wellness: Grow well.

5 Monetary adequacy: Find your wealth.

6 Quality of life (present): Seek peace.

7 Quality of life (future): Have dreams.

8 Spirituality/meaning: Construct purpose.

9 Respect for leisure: Have fun.

10 Personal flexibility: Welcome change.

11 Lifespan spiritual development: Live now.

12 Care-giving responsibilities: Honour yourself.

13 Home life: Get connected.

14 Maturation vitality: Become ageless.

15 Replacement of work functions: Get going.

With your own retirement success profile to hand, you will have solid proof of the relevance of the material to your own life. Since the profile describes you alone, you become concretely yet intimately aware that this learning is personal; the material isn't for the person sitting next to you, it is for you. And with the specific adult learning suggestions and learning activities that flow from your profile, you will immediately realise that the experience is individually practical.

Capitalising on inner strengths

You have been around for some time, picked up some valuable skills, and developed inner strengths, all of which you will now put to good use to ensure a happy and successful retirement. Among these inner strengths is one that is heightened by advancing years: the ability to harness mind power. Human mind power is awesome. We all live in a mind world, and how each of us conceives in our mind's eye what is happening in our world actually makes it so. You won't jump to conclusions nearly as readily as you might once have done, if you discipline yourself always to use mind power effectively by the continuous application of positive thought and action.

Maximising brain power to speed up self-actualisation

Your brain is equally awesome, more awesome than the most powerful computer ever invented or still to be conceived. It can translate into action all your ideas, and achieve your every scenario, ambition, and daydream. Those who know about such things reckon that on average we use only one tenth of this power in finding our way around life. How much more efficient we would all become by increasing this percentage by just another five points. Combine mind power (the catalyst) with brain power (the engine) and you will begin to close in on stretching the barriers.

In their book *Manage Your Mind* (Oxford University Press, 2003), authors Gillian Butler and Tony Hope list four keep-fit mental strategies that are smack in line with the retirement success strategies featured in this book.

o Clarify your goals and values.
o Manage your time.
o Study efficiently.
o Develop your full potential.

By adopting and using these keep-fit mental strategies, you will develop the skills and attitudes that enable you to lead a more fulfilling and productive life in your retirement years.

'Seven over 70'

The October 2003 edition of *Management Today* featured an article entitled 'Seven over 70', in which the contributor Rebecca Hoar reviewed the busy lifestyles of seven luminaries over the age of 70: Lika-Shing (75), Rupert Murdoch (72), Sir Kenneth Morrison (71), Queen Elizabeth II (77), Alan Greenspan (77), Bernie Ecclestone (72), and Liliane Bettencourt (78), the L'Oréal heiress. Rebecca reports:

None of us is getting any younger, but maybe in the world of work that doesn't matter as much as it used to. A mood swing is underway in the West: after a decade that ended in the ridiculous youth-led excesses of the dot.com boom, there is now a new respect – which has always been present in Eastern cultures – for the values of experience that greying hair brings. Under new legislation due to come into force in 2006, age limits on jobs will no longer be legal. Add to this the parlous state of pension schemes and the fact that it may become compulsory (or, at least, financially desirable) to work beyond the current retirement age, and it becomes clear that we should start treating the older generation with greater respect. Over-60s represent a huge and under-used repository of marketable skills, which forward-thinking employers ignore at their peril.

Food for thought for all up-and-coming retirees.

But ask yourself this: why are Rupert Murdoch, Alan Greenspan et al. still hacking it out there in the marketplace? They certainly don't need the money. Could it be that, like Lord Attenborough, they can't see purpose in retirement? Don't let this happen to you. When the time comes to let go, let go, and enjoy your new-found freedom in the third age. *You aren't retiring from life, just the full-time workplace.*

'Finding happiness in retirement'

Of equal significance in our quest for an enriching lifestyle is another pragmatic article, which first appeared in the *St Louis Dispatch*. It was written by Joanne Waldman, MEd, under the inspiring title 'Finding happiness in retirement'. Joanne debates:

Retirement is more complex than just receiving the gold watch and going off into the sunset. One of the factors comprising a successful retirement is Work Reorientation – the degree to which you have emotionally distanced yourself from taking your personal identity from work. In a lifetime, it is a natural process to disengage from work. However, it may be a very difficult process for those who primarily define themselves by their work or those who are workaholics. Redefining self without the benefit of a title is a frightening thought for many people. In social situations, and after an introduction, are you frequently asked 'What do you do?'

How will you answer that question once you are retired?

When you retire, it is necessary to shift your perspective from what you do to who you are. How can you move away from a definition of yourself based on your material accomplishments toward a growth definition of self? First, you could say that your worth isn't your work and still recognise your worthiness. Next, learn to put yourself first in order to discover your true self. The internal journey isn't easy and takes time along with self-introspection to come up with a new self-definition. Utilising the expertise of a retirement coach can be useful.

At 64, Tim felt that he wanted to start looking at his retirement options. Although not yet ready to retire, he was a self-described workaholic and knew that he was not prepared to successfully retire while still so engrossed with his work. He worked on getting to know himself again. Through written and verbal exercises and assessments, Tim spent time relearning and discovering his likes, dislikes, strengths and accomplishments. Then he began to design and set goals around his ideal retirement. He planned to phase into retirement by working full-time for a couple more years and then gradually decreasing his workload. During that time, he planned to explore new leisure pursuits, decide where to live in retirement, and to enjoy his grandchildren. Tim committed to learning how to slow down and live life to its fullest.

The idea of a gradual slowdown worked well for Tim, as he could not see himself stopping work one day without a plan to follow. In addition, he found his new definition of himself to be very empowering. He had more energy to try on new roles, learn new things and to pursue interests and dreams that had been lost in all those years of work.

Loss is a key element in all transition. In retirement, you may give up your role as a worker and redefine yourself from doing to being. Gradually accepting the loss and planning for retirement will make the transition easier for you.

So ask yourself these questions to see where you are in this process: To what degree do you feel that you have emotionally distanced yourself from your career? How much do you see your work as defining who you are? And how much of your personal worth is tied up in your work?

By answering these questions and exploring this issue, you are taking your first step toward your new retirement.

Backward glances

Glancing over your shoulder at what might have been is a waste of time, because what might have been is just that and no more. It *might* have been. As you enter into the glorious third age, you must put the past behind you and concentrate on the here and now; the only time you ever have. The pressure is off, responsibilities diminished, and the way open to achieving anything and everything you put your mind to.

Once retired, for most people it seems that there is a honeymoon phase of approximately 9 to 18 months, when time can be passed with leisure pursuits only. But then, from nowhere, comes the nagging question: 'Surely there must be more to life than this?' It is at this time that, unless pre-planning has been done well before the actual retirement date, uneasiness with life may set in.

Pre-retirement planning in all areas of life is essential, especially in this era of much earlier retirement. Today's demographics of many baby boomers retiring in their 50s over the next five to ten years opens up a whole future lifetime of possibilities and options. If you are recently retired or contemplating retirement, how will you deal with your new beginnings? Here is how.

1 Identify the keys to a happy and successful retirement.
2 Set goals for your new way of life.
3 Monitor progress with an audit checklist.
4 Devise a masterplan.
5 Go for it!

It's All Free for Seniors!

Finally, a little bonus I chanced upon as I was completing this chapter: a handy information manual for retirees, entitled *It's All Free for Seniors!* You won't find it in bookshops, because it is only procurable by mail order from the address below. Here is a preview of the core content.

o Get free prescriptions.
o Get free dental and eye care.
o Get income support without signing on.
o Get help paying your rent.
o Claim your council tax benefit.
o Keep warm in winter. (Cash is available for fuel bills.)
o Get free money to spruce up your home.
o Get the best solicitors to sort out legal problems for free.
o Get a budget loan to make a major purchase.
o Get help with the costs of travelling to see someone who is ill.
o Get cash to make your home draught-free this winter.
o Get cash to install security locks.
o Get an extra pension when you reach 80.
o Get free hearing aids and batteries.
o Get help with your phone bill.
o Visit your chiropodist for free.
o Get financial compensation if are mugged or burgled.
o Get free health care for your pets.
o Get a crisis loan in emergencies.
o Get help for disabled seniors.
o Fly anywhere at discounts of up to 90 per cent.

If you are as intrigued by the content as I was, you can get a copy of *It's All Free for Seniors!* by sending a cheque or postal order for £9.95 to Windsor Health, Emery House, Brunel Road, Southampton SO40 3SH.

Closing thoughts

There is life after work and hope in abundance, so take each day as it comes and never attempt tomorrow's tasks today. Keep active, and the ill-advised assertion that retirees 'eat half the day and sleep the other half' won't ever describe you. Above all, look after yourself; but be prepared for the odd shock. Just lately, the joints in my fingers have started to seize up one by one with the onset of arthritis, so I don't know how long I will be able to tap the keys as freely as I do now. C'est la vie. Maybe I could locate an online course on toe typing for digitally challenged retirees ...

And now, let me take my leave of you with my favourite quotation from my favourite author, Vernon Howard, who, during his lifetime, broke through to the higher plane and, 12 years after his death, continues to share his wisdom with countless millions: 'You have succeeded in life when all you really want is only what you really need.' May the life force flourish in all that you undertake in the glorious third age.

If you have a question, or would like to discuss any aspect of this book, feel free to contact me (jimgreen@writing-for-profit.com).

Useful reading

Ahuja, Ajay, *You, Your Property and Your Pension* (How To Books, 2004).

Brown, Rosemary, *Good Retirement Guide* (Kogan Page, 2002).

Claxton, John, *A Simple Guide to Pensions* (How To Books, 2002).

Green, Jim, *Starting Your Own Business* (How To Books, 2003)

Hare-Duke, Michael, *One Foot in Heaven* (SPCK, 2001).

Harrison, Debbie, *Wealth after Work* (Financial Times Prentice Hall, 2002).

Helen, Mary, *101 Secrets for a Great Retirement* (Shuford Smith, 2000).

Jones, Roger, *Retire Abroad* (How To Books, 2002).

Longhurst, Michael, *The Beginner's Guide to Retirement* (Newleaf, 2001).

Lowe, Jonquil, *The Which? Guide to Planning Your Pensions* (Which? Books, 2002).

Malaspina, Margaret A., *Don't Die Broke* (Bloomberg Press, 2001).

Orman, Suze and Mead, Linda, *You've Earned It, Don't Lose It* (Newmarket Press, 1997).

Power, Paul, *Starting Your Own Gardening Business* (How To Books, 2003).

Vice, Antony, *7 Ways to Beat the Pension Crisis* (How To Books, 2004).

Vice, Antony, *The Independent Pensioner* (Elliot Right Way Books, 2003).

White, John, *Investing in Stocks and Shares* (How To Books, 2003).

International retirement directory

UK organizations and resources

Advice and information

o Citizens' Advice Bureau (www.citizensadvice.org.uk).
  Free, confidential, and independent advice.
o Consumer Education (www.consumereducation.org.uk). A
  voluntary organisation that offers advice on a wide range
  of consumer issues.
o UK online (www.ukonline.gov.uk). Find your local council
  on this website.
o Which? (www.which.net/). The online version of the independent consumer guide.

Aged over 50

o Age Concern (www.ace.org.uk/). Has been providing help and support to the UK's elderly since 1943. The leading movement in the UK concerned with ageing and older people. Some offices run introductory web sessions.

o Age Exchange (www.age-exchange.org.uk/). In its 16th year, its work emerges from interviews with older people, now made available to a wider audience.

o AgeInfo (www.cpa.org.uk/ageinfo/ageinfo.html). An information service about old age and ageing, provided by the library and information service of the Centre for Policy on Ageing.

o Age-Net (www.age-net.co.uk/). An 'age-friendly' information and lifestyle website, which tries to cover all over-50s' interests, but is particularly strong on art and hobbies.

o Association of Retired and Persons Over 50 (www. arp050.org.uk). The UK's largest campaigning and social membership organisation for people over 50.

o Better Government for Older People (www.bgop.org.uk). Part of the government's modernisation agenda. Its learning network provides a range of interlinking services to local authority leaders, older people forums, and officers from local authorities.

o Centre for Policy on Ageing (www.cpa.org.uk/). A UK charity founded in 1947, which formulates and promotes social policies that enable older people to achieve their full potential in later years.

o Fifty Plus (http://fiftyplus.com) Links of special interest for retired people in the UK.

o Help the Aged (www.helptheaged.org.uk). A voluntary organisation focusing on the needs and concerns of elderly people.

o Laterlife (www.laterlife.com). A commercial website focusing on disparate retiree issues and interests.

o National Pensioners' Convention (www.natpencon. org.uk/). Declares that every pensioner has the right to choice, dignity, independence, and security as a valued member of society.

o Pensioners' Guide (www.info4pensioners.gov.uk/). Information on leisure, housing, home improvements, transport, legal services, and crime safety.

o Seniority (www.seniority.co.uk/). Launched on 1 June 2000 and aimed at the over-50s' online audience in the UK and beyond.

o Seniors' Network (www.scniorsnetwork.co.uk/). An information resource for older people and their organisations within the UK. The network supports the campaign for better pensions.

o Silverhairs (www.silverhairs.co.uk/). A technical helpline for senior surfers.

Education and training

o Basic Skills Agency (www.basic-skills.co.uk/). Provides assistance in obtaining basic skills, such as joinery, bricklaying, electrics, and arts and crafts.

o BBC Learning (www.bbc.co.uk/learning/). Offers a wide and disparate range of education facilities.

o British Educational Communications and Technology Agency (www.becta.org.uk/). A voluntary agency responsible for educational standards in information and communications technology.

o Campaign for Learning (www.campaign-for-learning. org.uk/). Sponsored and operated by a voluntary organisation.

o Hairnet (www.hairnet.org/). Internet training for the over-50s.

o learndirect (www.learndirect.co.uk/ or www.learndirects cotland.com/). The largest e-learning network in the UK. It allows people to learn at their local learndirect centre, or anywhere where they can get access to a computer and the internet.

o Learning and Skills Council (www.lsc.gov.uk/). Information on adult learning throughout the UK.

o Money to Learn (www.lifelonglearning.dfes.gov.uk/money tolearn/). The online version of a government booklet, which gives information on financial support for adult learners.

o National Grid for Learning (www.ngfl.gov.uk/). A government-sponsored facility.

o National Open College Network (www.nocn.org.uk). Aims to widen access to education for all adult learners.

o Open University (www.open.ac.uk/). A range of government-sponsored further education courses.

o People's Network (www.peoplesnetwork.gov.uk/). A government project that aims to make sure that every public library in the country is linked to the internet and has enough funding for computers.

o UK online centres (www.dfes.gov.uk/ukonlinecentres/). Give you the opportunity to use computers and get access to the internet in a supportive environment. You can find them in places like community centres, churches, schools, and libraries.

o University of the Third Age (www.u3a.org.uk). Offers a range of learning opportunities, delivered by older people for older people, including French, IT, music, history, art, and literature.

o WebWise (www.bbc.co.uk/webwise/learn/). A free online course for new web users.

o Workers' Educational Association (www.wea.org.uk/). A voluntary organisation controlling a wide range of workers' educational facilities.

Health and fitness

o Alzheimer's Society (www.alzheimers.org.uk). The official website for Alzheimer's sufferers, their families, and dependants.

o Carers Online (www.carersonline.org.uk). The official government website for UK carers and associated bodies.

o Diabetes UK (www.diabetes.org.uk/). The charity for people with diabetes.

o Disability Rights Commission (www.drc gb.org). Offers advice and support to the disabled.

o National Heart Forum (www.heartforum.org.uk/). Provides facts and current research about heart disease.

o NHS Cancer Screening Programmes (www.cancerscree ning.nhs.uk/). Information on the cancer screening programmes in England.

o NHS Direct (www.nhsdirect.nhs.uk). Your gateway to health information on the internet.

o Patient UK (www.patient.co.uk/showdoc.asp?doc=16). Lists UK websites that cover many aspects of health promotion and how to maintain a healthy lifestyle.

o Royal National Institute for the Blind (www.rnib.org.uk). Offers advice, support, and appliances for people with sight problems.

o Royal National Institute for the Deaf (www.rnid.org.uk). Offers advice, support, and appliances for the deaf and hard of hearing.

o Scotland Health (www.show.scot.nhs.uk/). Scottish National Health Service website devoted exclusively to health matters and issues of concern to the elderly.

o Scottish Sports Associations (www.scottishsportsassocia tion.org.uk/home/index.php). Lists all recognised sports associations in Scotland, together with details of activities.

o Sport England (www.sportengland.org/). The official government website for all recognised sports events in England, with details of facilities, venues, grants, and so on.

o Sport Scotland (www.sportscotland.org.uk/). The official government website for all recognised sports events in Scotland, with details of facilities, venues, grants, and so on.

o Sports Council for Wales (www.sports-council-wales.co.uk/index_flash.cfm?initapp=1). The official government website for all recognised sports events in Wales, with details of facilities, venues, grants, and so on.

o Walking the way to Health Initiative (www.whi.org.uk/). Contact the walking schemes starting up in your area.

o Your Weight (www.bbc.co.uk/health/yourweight/). This BBC website has tips and ideas to help you to achieve and maintain your healthy weight.

Humour

o Funmail (www.another.com). Your can now have a personalised email address for free. Up to 3,500 addresses are available, from motherinlaw.co.uk to blabbermouth.co.uk, summing up every emotion, mood, and occasion.

Media

o BBC Alert (www.bbc.co.uk). This is where you can make sure you don't miss any forthcoming BBC radio or TV programme that interests you. You may also register your interest and be notified by email.

o Later Life Magazines (www.laterlife.com/laterlife-magazines.htm) Includes magazines such as *SAGA* and *Choice*, aimed at the over-50s.

o *The Oldie* (www.theoldie.co.uk/). A lay-by of sanity on the information highway. The online website of *The Oldie* magazine was launched in 1992 by Richard Ingrams, former editor of *Private Eye*. Ingrams, who vowed he would never climb aboard the superhighway, does it better than most. It goes to show that content is more important than cables.

o Saga (www.saga.co.uk/publishing). The online version of Saga magazine includes general interest editorials, plus promotions for the group's own services.

o Third Age Press (www.thirdagepress.co.uk/). An independent publishing company providing materials to encourage fulfilment and continuing development after full-time employment.

o *Where to Retire* magazine (www.ontheweb.co.uk/uks/retire.html). Substantial discounts on hundreds of retiree magazines.

Online chat

o Age Concern Discussions (www.ageconcern.org.uk/discuss/). Browse or join in the conversations on these discussion boards.

o Baby Boomer Bistro (www.bbb.org.uk). You can join in online chat at this bistro run by Age Concern.

Tax and pensions

o Inland Revenue (www.inlandrevenue.gov.uk). The official government website for all matters relating to personal income tax liability.
o Pension Service (www.thepensionservice.gov.uk/home. asp). This arm of the Department for Work and Pensions has information for those approaching retirement, as well as for those already retired.

Volunteering

o Experience Corps (www.experiencecorps.co.uk). Aims to encourage a quarter of a million people aged 50 and over to volunteer to help develop their local communities.
o REACH (www.reach-online.org.uk). Recruits managerial or professional people no longer in full-time careers, and places them as volunteers throughout the UK.
o Retired and Senior Volunteer Programme (www.csv-rsvp.org.uk or www.csv-rsvpscotland.org.uk). Provides opportunities for people over 50 across the UK to become involved in their communities as volunteers.

Work

o Age Positive (www.agepositive.gov.uk/). Works with employers and employers' organisations to encourage the use of the government's voluntary code of practice on age diversity in employment.
o Guidance Council (www.guidancecouncil.com/). An independent campaigning organisation for career guidance in the UK.

- Jobcentre Plus (www.jobcentreplus.gov.uk). Brings together help in job-seeking and claiming benefits under one roof.
- New Deal 50 plus (www.newdeal.gov.uk/default.asp). Helps over-50s find the right job through one-to-one advice and financial support.
- New Deal for Disabled People (www.newdeal.gov.uk/new deal.asp?DealID=NDDIS). If you have a health condition or disability and are on a qualifying health-related benefit, New Deal for Disabled People can offer you access to a network of job brokers who offer support and advice to help you find work and stay in work.
- Third Age Employment Network (www.taen.org.uk/). A campaigning organisation committed to better opportunities for mature people to continue to learn, work, and earn. Works with the media, employers, and government to change attitudes and public policies.
- Wise Owls (www.wiseowls.co.uk). A web network for over-45s. Dedicated to promoting education and employment for this age group.
- Worktrain (www.worktrain.gov.uk). A government website listing national job opportunities.

Overseas organisations and resources

Australia

- About Seniors (www.aboutseniors.com.au/). The most comprehensive listing of information and links relevant to Australian senior citizens, veterans, retirees, those about to retire, pensioners, and carers.

o Adult Learning Australia (www.ala.asn.au/). A website for retiree education. Worth a look if you have relatives living in Aussie land.

o Australian Coalition '99 (http://home.vicnet.net.au/~ac99/index.html). A consortium of non-government organisations that promoted the International Year of the Older Persons 1999.

o Centre for Ageing Studies (www.cas.flinders.edu.au/). Promotes research into ageing.

o Council on the Ageing (www.cota.org.au/). Represents the interests of all Australians over 50.

o Endeavour Web (www.endeavour-web.org/). A Sydney-based website, designed, built, and managed by and for senior citizens.

o Office of Senior Interests (www.osi.wa.gov.au/). The mission is to enhance the lifestyles of seniors and encourage the community to plan for its ageing population.

o Older Women's Network (www.zip.com.au/~ownnsw/). Formed in 1985, when a number of women members and workers in the Combined Pensioners' Association decided that, although two-thirds of pensioners were women, there was little action or research around issues of particular concern to older women.

o SeniorNet (www.seniornet.com.au/). Helps seniors use computers and the internet.

Austria

o Katholisches Bildungswerk Wien (www.bildungswerk.at/). Provides education for older people.

Canada

o Babyboomers (www.suite101.com/welcome.cfm/baby_
boomers). A light-hearted boomer website within the
Suite101.com network of websites.

o 50More (www.50more.com/). An association for Canadians
over 50, it informs members about topics of interest, seeks
and publishes members' opinions, and obtains group discounts and special offers.

o Fifty-Plus Net (www.fifty-plus.net/). A network of Canadians over 50.

o Help the Aged Canada (www.helptheaged.ca/). Provides
help and assistance to low-income elderly people in Canada

Denmark

o Ældre Sagen (www.aeldresagen.dk/). The 'DaneAge Association' has more than 400,000 members. It influences
policies concerning older people in Denmark.

Europe

o European Centre for the Development of Vocational Training (www.cedefop.gr/). A European agency that promotes
vocational training in the European Union.

o European Research on the Education of Adults
(www.helsinki.fi/jarj/esrea/). Boosts research on the
education of adults in Europe through research networks,
conferences, and publications.

o European Union (europa.eu.int/index-en). An educational
website.

Finland

o Stakes (www.stakes.fi/cost219). A Finnish research institute active in the field of health and welfare for the disabled and the elderly.

France

o Cyberpapy (www.cyberpapy.com/). A website where grandparents can help children and grandchildren with their schoolwork.

o Fédération Internationale des petits frères des Pauvres (www.petits-freres.org/). The 'International Federation of Little Brothers of the Poor' provides assistance for the elderly.

o Seniorplanet.fr (www.senior-planet.com/). A website for senior citizens.

Germany

o NETclub 50+ (www.netclub.at/senioren). A network for the over-50s.

o SeniorenNet (www.seniorennet.de/). An international non-profit organisation that educates older adults in computer technology.

Holland

o Global Seniors (www.geocities.com/globalseniors). A conversational group for people aged 50 and over worldwide. Communicating thoughts in friendship and achieving a mutual understanding are the primary goals.

o National Age Discrimination Office (www.leeftijd.nl/ update/english.html). Information on the work of the pioneering office.

o SeniorWeb (www.seniorweb.nl/gb/intro.asp). A website by and for senior citizens.

o TNO Centre for Ageing Research (www.ageing.tno.nl/). Conducts research-and-development projects relating to the over-50s.

India

o HelpAge India (www.helpageindia.com). A member organisation of Help the Aged.

Ireland

o Irish Pension Market (www.uk-insurance-directory.com/ links/pensionsuk.html). Annuities, phased retirement and income.

Malta

o Prehistory of Malta (www.catal.arch.cam.ac.uk/temper/ doc_view.asp?doc_id=83). Pensioner-students studying the prehistory of Malta are finding themselves useful in life even after retirement.

New Zealand

o Grey Power (www.greypower.co.nz/). Promotes the welfare and well-being of citizens in the over-50 group.

Sweden

o SeniorNet Sweden (www.seniornet.se). Committed to making IT available to all Swedish senior citizens.

Switzerland

o Computeria St Gallen (www.goeast.ch/computeria). Runs local computer courses.

US

o Administration on Ageing (www.aoa.gov). US retirees remain active and healthy as they age.
o Agenet (www.agenet.com/). An information and referral network designed to bridge the gap between ageing parents and adult children.
o American Association of Retired Persons (www.aarp.org/). Provides members with benefits and discounts, as well as advice and information.
o American Home Guides (www.americanhomeguides.com/). Master-planned communities, active retirement communities.
o Boomers' International (http://boomersint.org/). An extensive and lively website, which is full of fun and information.
o Elderhostel (www.elderhostel.org/). A non-profit organisation that provides educational travel opportunities.
o Elderweb (www.elderweb.org/). An online community of older US computer users.
o 50 Plus (www.50plus.org/). Aims to motivate people aged 50 and over to take exercise.

o 50 Plus Expeditions (www.50plusexpeditions.com/is). An adventure travel company that specialises in active trips to exotic destinations for people aged 50 and over. Small groups (maximum 16 travellers). The tours go beyond conventional sightseeing packages and reach out to the people and environment of a country.

o Friendly 4 Seniors (www.friendly4seniors.com/). Lists useful websites for seniors.

o Geezer Brigade (www.thegeezerbrigade.com/). An international organisation by and for 'Seniors with an Attitude' – those over 55 who have not given up the ghost or lost their sense of humour.

o Grandma Betty (www.grandmabetty.com/). Developed by an active senior for active seniors.

o Learning Resources Network (www.lern.org). Resources for the elderly.

o Lovin' Life News (www.wwseniors.com/). The online version of a long-established, large-circulation senior newspaper in Arizona.

o National Ageing Information Centre (www.aoa.dhhs.gov/naic). Gives access to databases, statistics, and publications on ageing.

o New York State Office for the Aging (http://aging.state.ny.us/index.htm). Serves older New Yorkers and their families online.

o Over The Hill Gang International (http://www.othgi.com/). A unique ski club for the over-50s, with than 6,000 members in the US and 13 other countries, including the UK. Publishes a regular newsletter with information on trips, member benefits, equipment, and skier fitness. Offers discounts on lift passes, lessons, accommodation, and travel.

o Retirement Source Book (www.all-garden-books.com/ 0737300396.htm). Answers to lots of decisions, opportunities and challenges that accompany the retirement journey.

o SeniorCom (www.senior.com/). Supplies products, services, information, and entertainment for the over-50s.

o Senior Information Network (www.senior-inet.com/). Provides information about senior support services across the US.

o SeniorLaw (www.seniorlaw.com/). Resources on law concerning the elderly.

o SeniorLiving (www.seniorliving.com). The Senior's guide in the about.com network of websites.

o SeniorNet (www.seniornet.org/). A non-profit organisation that provides computer access and training to people over 50 across the US.

o Senior Surfers (www.seniorsurfers.org/). News, views, and resources for seniors and their carers.

o Suddenly Senior (www.suddenlysenior.com/). A weekly e-zine and humour column that speaks to the hearts and funny bones of everyone over 50 who became senior before their time.

o ThirdAge (www.thirdage.com/). An extensive range of innovative ideas, information, and services, superbly presented in a lively and entertaining style.

o United Seniors' Association (www.unitedseniors.org/). Works to protect the retirement security of Americans.

o WidowNet (www.fortnet.org/WidowNet). An information and self-help resource by and for widows and widowers.

o Woman of a Certain Age Page (www.womanofacertainag epage.com). An e-zine for feisty women over 40.

Worldwide

o Commonwealth of Learning (www.col.org/). A Commonwealth agency dedicated to the promotion of distance learning and open learning.

o HelpAge International (www.helpage.org/). Lists the worldwide network of member organisations of Help the Aged.

o United Nations Population Information Network (www.un. org/popin/). A guide to population information on United Nations websites.

Travel

Hotels

Wherever you wish to book a hotel bed, be it for one night or two weeks, you won't find it hard to book. Some websites give you a virtual guided tour.

o AA (www.theaa.com). An easy-to-use website. You can search by destination name or click on the map of the UK to find hotels in a particular area.

o All Rooms (www.all-rooms.com). Hotel, bed-and-breakfast, and discount accommodation in the UK, Europe, and the US, including hotel accommodation at all major international airports.

- Celtic Castles (www.celticcastles.com). You can book rooms in a number of Scottish castles here. Look at the map of Scotland and click on the area you want to visit, in order to find a castle to stay in.
- Corus and Regal Hotels (www.corushotels.co.uk/). Hotels in the UK, Australia, and Malaysia.
- Grand Heritage Hotels (www.grandheritage.com). Choose from hotels in the UK, mainland Europe, the Caribbean, and North America.
- Harmony Suites St Lucia (www.harmonysuites.com). A hotel on the scenic waterfront of exclusive Rodney Bay, just 200 yards from St Lucia's famous Reduit Beach. Managed by a local British and St Lucian family. A beautiful hotel in a warm and intimate atmosphere.
- Hotel Guide (www.hotelguide.com). Hotel rooms available throughout the world. An attractive, easy-to-use website, with discounts for online bookings and some special deals.
- Hotels Travel (www.hotelstravel.com). An extensive database of hotel rooms throughout the world that can be booked online. The website also gives links to airlines and car-hire companies.
- Jarvis Hotels (www.jarvis.co.uk). An easy-to-use website. Type in the destination, dates, and number of people, and the website will give you a list of hotels available.
- Johansens (www.johansens.com). The finest hotels, country houses, traditional inns, châteaux, and resorts throughout the world.
- RAC (www.rac.co.uk). A good search facility for hotels. The website also has details of special offers.

Flights

Bargain flights are always available. There is lots of choice, so shop around.

o Air-Flights (www.air-flights.co.uk). Flights to Malaga, Alicante, Tenerife, and other European destinations.

o air 2000 (www.air2000.com). Charter flights with air 2000 or schedule flights with Unijet.

o British Airways (www.britishairways.com). As well as being able to book online, you can check special offers and flight information.

o Buzz (www.openjet.com). A low-cost airline offering good deals.

o Cheap Flights (www.cheapflights.com). A good choice of searches, with some last-minute deals.

o Cheap Online Flights (www.cheaponlineflights.com). Search and book online.

o Cheep Flights (www.cheepflights.com). Yes, that is how it is spelt. The website has two types of pricing and a booking engine.

o Destinations (www.destinations.co.uk). An easy-to-use website that has discounted fares and a useful world travel guide.

o easyJet (www.easyjet.com). Book online with this easy-to-use website. A low-cost no-frills airline.

o ebookers (www.ebookers.com). Flights worldwide.

o Expedia (www.expedia.co.uk). This website allows you to check flight timetables, in addition to booking flights online.

o Farebase (www.farebase.co.uk). You can check prices for both charter and schedule flights on this website.

o Flightfile (www.flightfile.com). Likewise, you can check prices for both charter and schedule flights here.

o Flightline (www.flightline.co.uk). This website offers both charter and schedule flights, as well as airport parking, holidays, and holiday insurance.

o Flightsdirect (www.flightsdirect.com). You can check prices for both charter and schedule flights on this website.

o Flights4Less (www.flights4less.co.uk). Discount tickets and cheap flights from the UK, with fares from over 60 airlines to destinations worldwide.

o Global Directions (www.globaldirections.co.uk). An easy-to-use search facility.

o Just Flights (www.just-flights.co.uk). A search facility for both charter and schedule flights.

o 1 Call Flights (www.1callflights.com). Search online, then phone to book.

o Premier Leisure (www.premier-leisure-flights.com). Charter flights available on this website.

o Rainbow Flights (www.rainbow-flights.co.uk). Bargain flights worldwide.

o Ryanair (www.ryanair.com). A basic website, but easy to use. Book online. Cheap no-frills flights to Europe.

o Travel Brand (www.thetravelbrand.com). Charter flights only.

o Travel Data (www.traveldata.co.uk). An easy-to-use search facility. The website also has information on a good number of destinations.

o Travelselect (www.engb.lastminute.com). Specialises in late availability. Also offers European, Caribbean, North American, and business-class deals.

Airports

Check flight information and availability at these UK and Irish airports.

o Aberdeen: Phone 01224 722331.

o Belfast: Phone 028 9448 4848.

o Birmingham: Phone 0121 767 5511.

o Blackpool: Phone 01253 343434.

o Bournemouth: Phone 01202 364000.

o Bristol: Phone 0870 12 12 747.

o Cardiff: Phone 01446 711111.

o Cork: Phone 00 353 21 4313 131.

o Edinburgh: Phone 0131 333 1000.

o Glasgow: Phone 0141 887 1111.

o Glasgow Prestwick: Phone 01292 511000.

o Humberside: Phone 01652 688456.

o Isle of Man: Phone 01624 821600.

o Leeds/Bradford: Phone 0113 250 9696.

o Liverpool: Phone 0151 288 4000.

o London City: Phone 020 7646 0088.

o London Gatwick: Phone 0870 000 2468.

o London Heathrow: Phone 0870 0000 123.

o London Stanstead: Phone 0876 0000 303.

o Manchester: Phone 0161 489 3000.

o Newcastle: Phone 0191 489 3000.

o Shannon: Phone 00 353 6 1 712400.

o Sheffield: Phone 0114 201 1998.

o Southampton: Phone 023 8062 0021.

o Teeside: Phone 01325 332811.

Ferries

An affordable way of getting to the continent.

o Britanny Ferries (www.britanny-ferries.com). Ferry prices, with online booking and ferry schedules, on this website.

- Ferrysavers (www.ferrysavers.co.uk). Short sea crossings to Ostend, Dieppe, Dublin, and Rosslare are covered on this website.
- Hoverspeed (www.hoverspeed.co.uk). Lots of information. You can choose your route with schedules and fares, and book online. The website also has details of short breaks and special offers.
- P & O North Sea Ferries (www.ponsf.com). Travel from Hull to Zeebrugge or Rotterdam with P & O. The website gives information on fares and special offers.
- P & O Stena Line (www.posl.com). Good information on this website, including timetable and online booking.
- Sea France (www.seafrance.co.uk). A very informative website, including an instant fare calculator. You put in details of the crossing, number of travellers, and car (if any), and the website will give you the fare. There are also details of sailings and special offers.
- Sea View (www.seaview.co.uk). This website gives details of ferry operators, savers, and route guides.

Trains

An easy way of getting to the continent. Eurostar is well worth a try.

- Anglia Railways (www.angliarailways.co.uk). An easy-to-use website, with good information. You can book online. If you book by 7.00 p.m. on Monday–Friday or 12 noon on Saturdays, you will receive your tickets by first-class post, so you don't have to queue. There is a handy journey planner on the website.
- British Rail (www.britrail.co.uk). Information on time-tables and where to buy your tickets.

o Eurostar (www.eurostar.com). You can book tickets online for the high-speed Channel Tunnel trains.

o First North Western (www.firstnorthwestern.co.uk). This website has timetables, route maps, and a journey planner.

o Great Western Trains (www.great-western-trains.co.uk). An attractive, easy-to-use website, with information on times, fares, and online booking.

o Heathrow Express (www.heathrowexpress.co.uk). You can check times and fares, and book tickets online. There is information about luggage check-in and customers with special needs, as well as Heathrow arrivals and schedules.

o South West Trains (www.swtrains.co.uk). An informative, easy-to-use website, with details of times, booking, airport links, and travel offers.

o Thames Trains (www.thamestrains.co.uk). Up-to-date information about times and engineering work, and an online booking form.

o Trainline (www.thetrainline.com). Book tickets and reserve seats for any train operator in the UK.

o Transport for London (www.londontransport.co.uk/tfl/). Detailed information on transport services in London, including bus, tube, and river services. There is also information on tickets and maps.

o UK Railways on the Net (www.rail.co.uk). This website has links to train-operating companies, timetables on the internet, and a travel bureau with tourist information.

o Virgin Trains (www.virgintrains.co.uk). You can book online on this website, and there are some discounts for booking in this way. The website also has information on times for all trains.

Car hire

Try these European and worldwide car hire companies.

o Avis (www.avis.co.uk). A hire guide, online booking, and special offers.

o Car Hire Direct (www.carhiredirect.co.uk). An easy-to-use search facility. Worldwide car hire.

o Car Hire Group (www.carhire.co.uk). Low-cost worldwide car hire.

o Car Hire Online (www.carhire-online.co.uk). Book online or by phone.

o Direct Car Hire (www.direct-car-hire.co.uk). Save money by booking directly with Direct Car Hire, and avoid paying commission charged by travel agents – so the website says.

o Dollar (www.dollar.co.uk). Car hire for the US.

o Europcar (www.europcar.co.uk). Online quotes and reservations.

o Hertz (www.hertz.co.uk). Easy to use. Book a car to use all over the world.

o Park and Go (www.parkandgo.co.uk). Easy to use. You can book car parking, as well as car hire.

o Thrifty Car Hire (www.thrifty.co.uk). Get a quote online for overseas reservations.

Hobbies

Aquariums

o Fishkeeping UK (www.fishkeepinguk.co.uk). An extensive directory of national associations, importers, retailers, and web-based clubs.

Art

o Teaching Art (www.teachingart.co.uk). A leading producer of art training videos.

Astronomy

o Beacon Hill Telescopes (www.beaconhilltelescopes.mcmail.com). One of the UK's leading suppliers of astronomical equipment, offering a large selection and low prices.
o Cosmicdust (www.cosmicdust.com). A diary of celestial events to help you plan stargazing with ease, without equipment even.
o UK250 (www.uk250.co.uk). Find out about the world of astronomy and learn what you need to become an amateur stargazer.

Bridge

o Card Games (www.pagat.com). Explains the rules of play for rubber, duplicate, and Chicago bridge.
o English Bridge Union (www.ebu.co.uk). The website for an experienced player thinking of entering tournaments, who wants to know the exact rules of bridge.

Collecting

o Collector Online (www.collectoronline.com). The most complete listing on collectors' clubs.

Crosswords

o Crossword Compiler (www.crosswordcompiler.com). Instruction on developing your own crosswords.

o Crossword Directory (http://home.freeuk.net/dharrison/ puzzles/). Provides puzzles and forums.

o One Across (www.oneacross.com). Provides suggestions for solving puzzles.

o Questique (www.questique.co.uk). A strategy crossword game for up to four players. A simple handicapping system allows children and adults to compete as equals.

Digital photography

o Image Acquire (www.image-acquire.com). Reviews the latest digital cameras.

o ShortCourses (www.shortcourses.com). Digital photography courses.

Fishing

o Where to Fish (www.where-to-fish.com). Devoted to finding the best fishing spots worldwide.

Gardening

o The Garden (www.thegarden.co.uk). Boasts an impressive list of services: hints and tips in the 'Shed', a retail and wholesale directory in the 'Nursery', and information on gardening services and products in 'Services'.

Genealogy

o Family Search (www.familysearch.org). Hosts a world-wide database of births, deaths, and marriages.

o One Name (www.one-name.org). Specialises in tracing the history of a particular surname, and has links to groups that can help you make searches.

o UK Genealogy (www.ukgenealogy.uk). The portal for UK genealogical research. It can source records of ancestors via a number of websites.

Graphology

o British Institute of Graphology (www.britishgraphology. org). Contains information about tuition, as well as helpful links.

o Handwriting Analysis (www.handwriting.org). Promotes awareness, understanding, and support for handwriting analysis, and provides a central source of information.

History

o Leisure Learning (www.bbc.co.uk/history/). If you are interested in medieval history, then take a look at this website.

Home-brewing

o Tom and Vince's Homebrew Site (www.alpha-byte. demon.co.uk). The pages are designed to help you learn the basics of home-brewing, as well as advanced skills and how to produce top-quality home brew.

Juggling

o Juggling (www.juggling.org). The main website for jugglers on the internet. It has listings for clubs, societies, events, magazines, and software. Most importantly, it has lessons on how to juggle clubs, balls, hoops, and anything else you can think of.

Kites

o Clem's Kites (www.clem.freeserve.co.uk). Learn how to make some great kites from nothing but newspaper, tape, and string.
o Kiteworld (www.kiteworld.co.uk). The home of kite-flying on the Net.

Model-making

o Hobbies (Dereham) Limited (www.hobbies-dereham.co.uk). This company supplies a vast range of toys and model-making equipment worldwide through the famous Hobbies Handbook. You can order any product from the website.

Puppeteering

o No Strings Attached Online (www.mimicsproductions.co.uk). Gives details of how to design and produce your own puppets and stages in different styles, as well as providing links to other useful websites and how to book this puppet group for shows.

Radio

o Radio Society of Great Britain (www.rsgb.org.uk). The UK's internationally acclaimed society for all radio amateurs.

Writing

o Arvon Foundation (www.arvonfoundation.org). Runs inexpensive one-week residential writing courses at inspiring locations in Devon, Yorkshire, and Scotland. The courses cover the writing of fiction, poetry, travelogue, and screenplays.

o Dan Poynter's Para Publishing (www.parapublishing. com). Gives guidance on every aspect of publishing, including self-publishing.

o Mystery Writers' Forum (www.ideas4writers.co.uk/ public/ideas/mystery.php). Provides information on forensics, poisons, guns, and other topics that will help you get your facts right.

o Trace Project (www.trace.ntu.ac.uk). Run by Nottingham University, this project focuses on online writing.

o Writing for Profit (www.writing-for-profit.com). A resource centre for writers aspiring to publication in the realms of niche non-fiction. Tutorials, tools, tips, techniques, and free instructional e-books are provided.

Internet

Search engines

o Ask (www.ask.com). A popular search engine for general enquiries.

o Google (www.google.com). The most popular and efficient search engine of all. It houses billions of topics, websites, and articles.

o Looksmart (www.looksmart.com). Not as prominent as it once was, but still useful for general search terms.

o MSN (www.msn.com). A multi-purpose website that uses Hotmail as its consumer email provider.

o Yahoo (www.yahoo.com). Until recently Yahoo fed off Google resources, but now it has its own comprehensive database. It also provides free email addresses.

o Yahoo for Seniors (http://seniors.yahoo.com/). The major search engine for all matters relating to retirement. A directory devoted exclusively to worldwide retiree interests.

Index